¡Viva el español!

Workbook

System B

John De Mado
Linda West Tibensky
Patti Lozano

Jane Jacobsen-Brown
Christine Wolinski Szeszol
Donna Alfredo Wardanian

Marcela Gerber, Series Consultant

Wright Group

www.WrightGroup.com

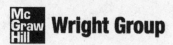
Wright Group

Send all inquiries to:
Wright Group/McGraw-Hill
P.O. Box 812960
Chicago, Illinois 60681

ISBN: 0-07-602964-6

18 19 20 21 22 23 QVS 23 22 21 20 19

Contenido

Contenido

Lección 1

¡Vamos a la clase de español!

Yo hablo

Listen to the questions. Then answer them based on your own experience.

1. ¿Cómo te llamas? _____

2. ¿Cómo se llama tu papá? _____

3. ¿Cuántos años tienes? _____

4. ¿Cuántos pupitres hay en el salón de clases? _____

5. ¿Cuántos lápices tienes? _____

6. ¿Dónde está tu nariz? _____

7. ¿Dónde están tus ojos? _____

8. ¿Tienes un gato? _____

9. ¿Tienes frío? _____

10. ¿Tienes miedo de las gallinas? _____

Yo practico

A. Look at the picture. Circle the items as the teacher reads them to you.

B. Match the words on the left with the pictures on the right. Draw a line to connect them.

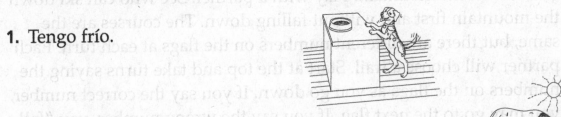

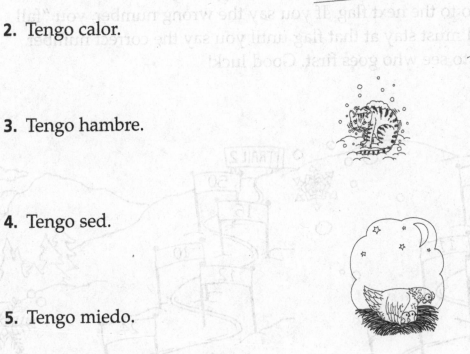

1. Tengo frío.

2. Tengo calor.

3. Tengo hambre.

4. Tengo sed.

5. Tengo miedo.

6. Tengo sueño.

7. Tengo dolor.

8. Tengo prisa.

9. Tengo suerte.

Yo juego

A. Race down the mountain. Play with a partner. See who can ski down the mountain first and without falling down. The courses are the same, but there are different numbers on the flags at each turn. Each partner will choose a trail. Start at the top and take turns saying the numbers on the flags as you go down. If you say the correct number, you may go to the next flag. If you say the wrong number, you "fall down" and must stay at that flag until you say the correct number. Flip a coin to see who goes first. Good luck!

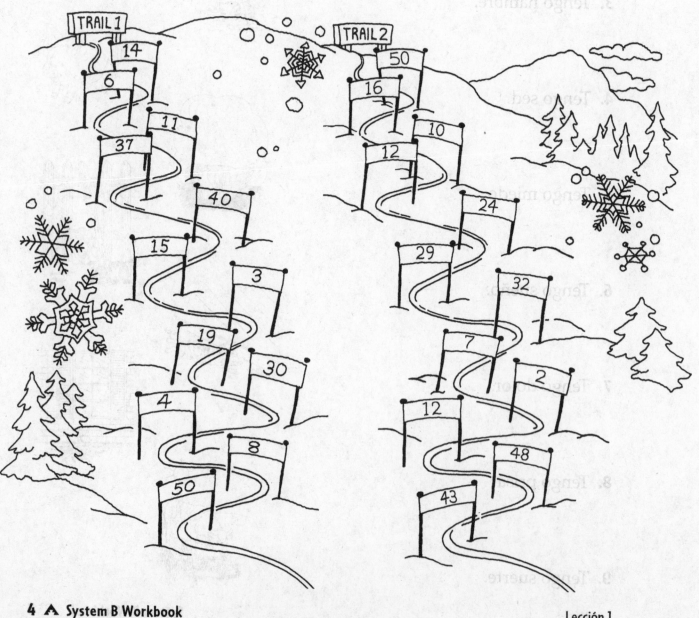

B. There are sixteen classroom objects hidden in this picture. Can you find them? Circle the hidden objects you find.

Lección 2

¡Vamos a aprender más español!

Yo hablo

Your friend Antonio is very curious. He asks a lot of questions! Think about what he asks. Then answer his questions.

1. ¿Qué día de la semana es hoy? _____

2. ¿Qué fecha es hoy? _____

3. ¿Cuándo es tu cumpleaños? _____

4. ¿Qué llevas hoy? _____

5. ¿Qué tiempo hace? _____

6. ¿Qué tiempo hace en enero? _____

7. ¿Qué llevas en enero? _____

8. ¿Adónde vas cuando hace buen tiempo? _____

9. ¿Qué haces cuando está lloviendo? _____

10. ¿Cómo se llama el director o la directora de la escuela?

_____

Yo practico

A. Finish the faces to show how these people feel today.

Estoy contenta.

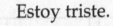

Estoy triste.

Estoy enojada.

B. Amalia was very forgetful this week. She lost her ruler, pencil, sweater, jacket, socks, shoes, book, and sunglasses in school! Help her find the items by circling them in the pictures. Then take turns with a classmate to ask and answer questions about where each item is.

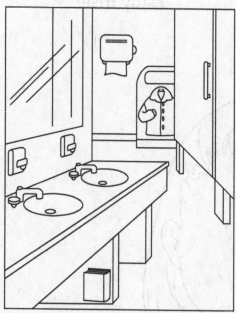
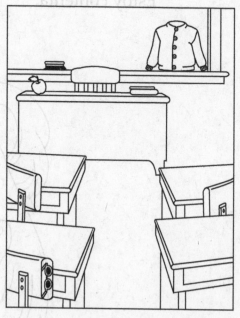

Yo imagino

A. Listen to the description of this scene. Then draw a picture to describe what you hear. Share your picture with the class.

(1) Hace buen tiempo. Hace calor y hace sol. Hay una escuela. Hay una bandera americana. El maestro habla con un niño y una niña. (2) El niño está muy bien. Él lleva pantalones, una camisa y zapatos. Él tiene una regla y un globo. (3) La niña está muy mal. Ella lleva una falda, una blusa, calcetines y zapatos. ¡Ella tiene siete libros! (4) También hay un parque grande. Un niño y una niña juegan al tenis. Ellos llevan una camiseta y pantalones cortos. Un niño nada en la piscina. Una niña salta la cuerda.

B. Have you ever seen a funny-looking creature with two heads and six feet? Well, your teacher has! Listen as your teacher describes the creature. Then draw a picture of what you hear to find out what else the creature has.

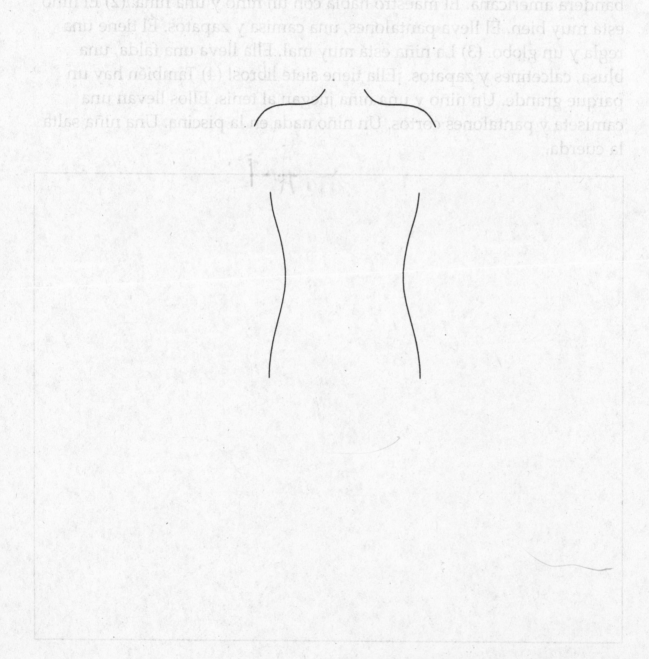

Lección 3

¡Vamos a mirar nuestra casa!

Yo aprendo el vocabulario

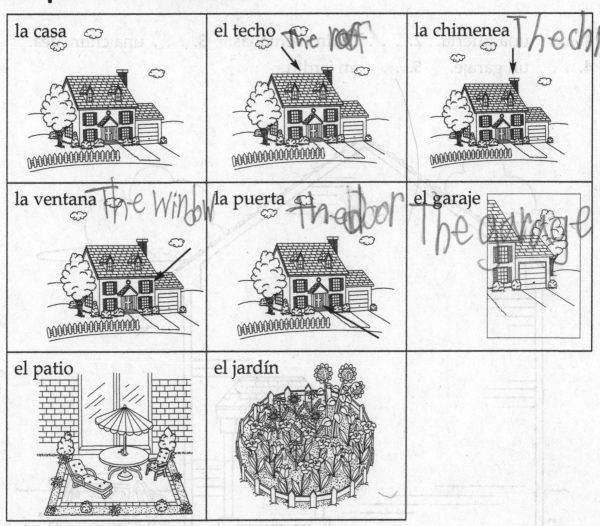

la casa	el techo *The roof*	la chimenea *The chimney*
la ventana *The window*	la puerta *The door*	el garaje *The garage*
el patio	el jardín	

Más vocabulario

¿Qué tiene la casa? La casa tiene _____.

¿Cuántas (Cuántos) _____ hay en la casa?

Hay _____.

Yo hablo

Darío is drawing a house. Help him complete his drawing by adding the missing parts according to the information given below.

La casa tiene . . .

1. . . . una puerta. **2.** . . . cuatro ventanas. **3.** . . . una chimenea.

4. . . . un garaje. **5.** . . . un jardín.

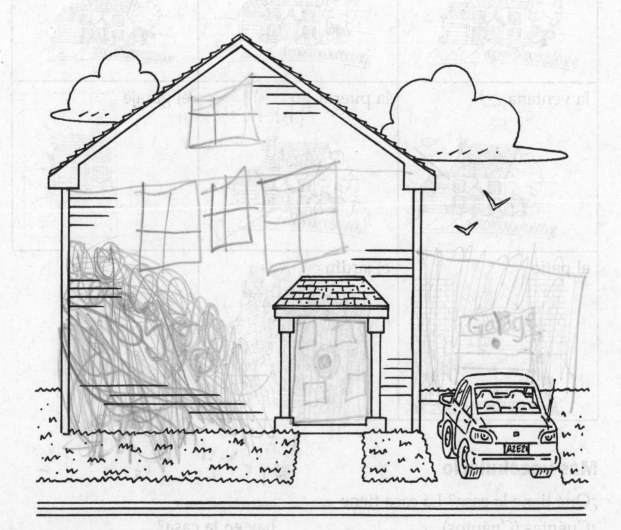

Yo practico

Marina is telling you about her house. It's very colorful! Follow her instructions to color the house. Then answer the questions below.

- El techo es rojo.
- Las ventanas son azules.
- El garaje es amarillo.
- El patio es gris.

- Las chimeneas son anaranjadas.
- La puerta es marrón.
- El jardín es verde y rosado.

1. ¿Cuántas ventanas hay en la casa? _Hay ocho ventanas azules._

2. ¿Cuántas puertas hay en la casa? _Hay estas_

3. ¿Cuántos techos hay en la casa? _una_

4. ¿Cuántos garajes hay en la casa? _garages_

5. ¿Cuántas chimeneas hay en la casa? _dos chimeneas_

6. ¿Cuántos patios hay en la casa? _cero patios_

7. ¿Cuántos jardines hay en la casa? _una jardines_

Yo juego

Start at the beginning of the maze and find your way from house to house until you reach the end. Describe each house you come to. You might say something like, **"La casa tiene una ventana. La casa no tiene jardín."**

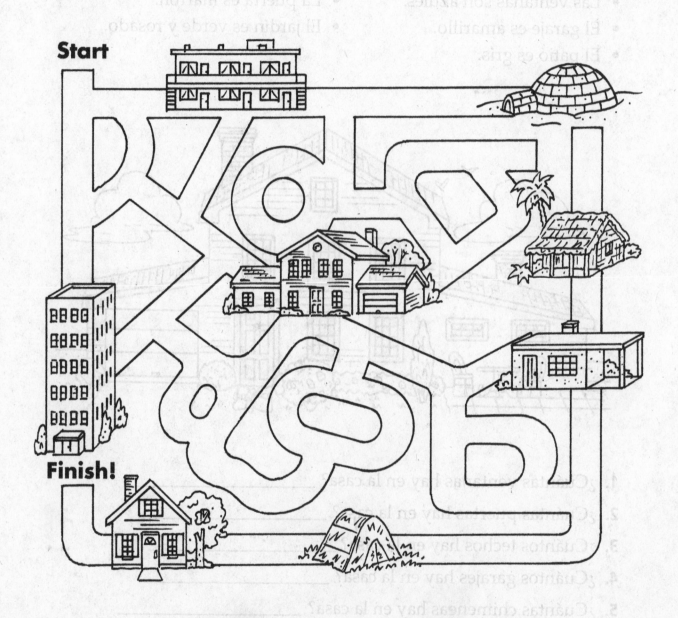

Yo juego

Negrín, the cat, is sleeping comfortably on the bed. That is until Marcos, the dog, starts chasing her around the house! Listen to the sentences and draw a line from one room to the next to follow Negrín's path.

1. El gato corre a la sala.

2. El gato corre al comedor.

3. El gato corre al dormitorio.

4. El gato corre a la cocina.

5. El gato corre al sótano.

6. El gato corre al ático.

7. El gato corre al jardín.

8. El gato corre al techo.

9. El gato corre al patio.

Yo imagino

Imagine that you could design your own house. What would it look like? Draw and color a picture of your dream house. Include your family and pets inside your house. Don't forget to include yourself!

Lección 5

Vamos a contar hasta sesenta

Yo aprendo el vocabulario

cincuenta y uno	51
cincuenta y dos	52
cincuenta y tres	53
cincuenta y cuatro	54
cincuenta y cinco	55
cincuenta y seis	56
cincuenta y siete	57
cincuenta y ocho	58
cincuenta y nueve	59
sesenta	60

Más vocabulario

¿Cuántos es _____ más _____?

Yo hablo

Everyone has questions! Think about how you would answer these.

1. ¿Cuántos niños hay en tu clase? _____

2. ¿Cuántos libros hay en tu dormitorio? _____

3. ¿Cuántos lápices hay en tu salón de clases? _____

4. ¿Cuántas sillas hay en la cafetería de la escuela? _____

5. ¿Cuánto es diecinueve más treinta y siete? _____

6. ¿Cuánto es veinticinco más veintiséis? _____

7. ¿Cuánto es veintisiete más treinta y uno? _____

8. ¿Cuánto es treinta más treinta? _____

9. ¿Cuánto es veinte más treinta y cinco? _____

Yo practico

Julia is on her way to her friend Olivia's house, but she forgot her glasses and she can't see the house numbers. Look at the houses and answer her questions.

1. ¿Qué número tiene la casa con el jardín? _____

2. ¿Qué número tiene la casa con once ventanas? _____

3. ¿Qué número tiene la casa con dos chimeneas? _____

4. ¿Qué número tiene la casa con una ventana? _____

5. ¿Qué número tiene la casa con el techo negro? _____

6. ¿Qué número tiene la casa con una chimenea y tres ventanas?

_____

Yo juego

You are hiking in the jungle. As you walk down the path, you must pass many wild animals by saying the corresponding numbers in a loud, clear voice. Play alone or with a friend. Who can hike all the way through the forest without stopping?

Yo imagino

At the Annual Artist Alphabet contest, each artist must draw a picture only of things that start with the letter on his or her easel. Choose a letter between *a* and *m* and write it on your easel. Then draw pictures of objects that start with this letter. Last, take turns with your classmates to point to the objects you drew and say their names.

Lección **6**
¿Qué hay en los cuartos?

Yo aprendo el vocabulario

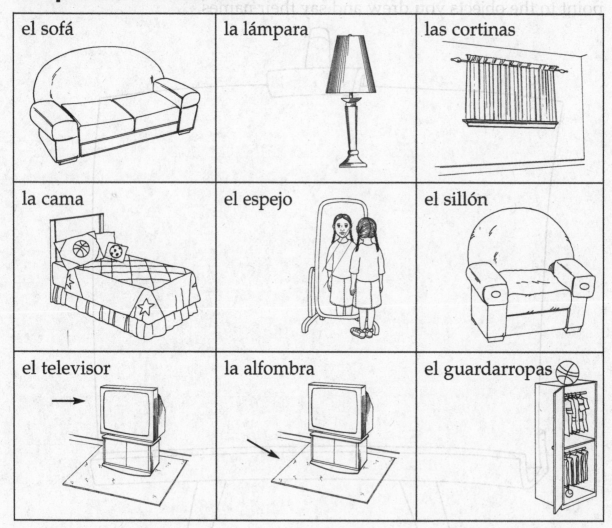

el sofá	la lámpara	las cortinas
la cama	el espejo	el sillón
el televisor	la alfombra	el guardarropas

Yo practico

A. Your cousin Ángela is coming to spend a week at your house. She wants to know where everything is in your house. She also wants to know the color of some things. Answer her questions.

1. ¿Dónde está tu cama? _Mi casa esta en el dormitorio._

2. ¿De qué color es tu cama? _Mi cama es rojo._

3. ¿Dónde hay un sofá en tu casa? _Mi sofa es cafe._

4. ¿De qué color es el sofá? _____

5. ¿Dónde hay un espejo en tu casa? _____

6. ¿Dónde está el televisor en tu casa? _Mi televisor esta en la sala._

7. ¿Dónde hay una alfombra en tu casa? _____

8. ¿De qué color es la alfombra? _____

9. ¿Dónde hay cortinas en tu casa? _____

10. ¿De qué color son las cortinas? _____

B. María and her friends are all looking for something. Circle the picture that best describes what each person is looking for based on the situation.

1. María tiene sueño.
Ella busca

5. Adriana tiene sed.
Ella busca

2. Es de noche y José tiene miedo.
Él busca

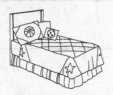 

6. Carmela quiere ver una película.
Ella busca

 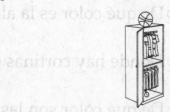

3. Ramona tiene hambre.
Ella busca

 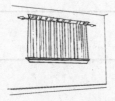

7. Gonzalo necesita un suéter.
Él busca

4. Javier tiene dolor de los pies.
Él busca

8. Rodrigo quiere ver la televisión en la sala.
Él busca

 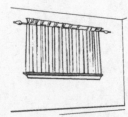

Yo imagino

The Alonso family is moving into their new house today! But the movers are taking a lunch break, and they left all the furniture on the sidewalk. Draw the furniture in the empty rooms, where you think it should go. Color your picture. Describe your picture to the class.

Lección 7
Hacer los quehaceres

Yo aprendo el vocabulario

la estufa	el horno	el microondas
el lavaplatos	el refrigerador	el fregadero
la lavadora	la secadora	

Más vocabulario

Pongo _____ en _____.

Saco _____ de _____.

Yo hablo

Your aunt Beatriz wants to buy an anniversary gift for your parents. She wants to know about some of the things you have in your house. She also wants to know the color of some things. Answer her questions.

1. ¿De qué color es tu refrigerador? _____

2. ¿Hay un lavaplatos en tu casa? _____

3. ¿Hay una secadora en tu casa? _____

4. ¿Dónde está el fregadero en tu casa? _____

5. ¿Hay una lavadora en tu casa? _____

6. ¿Hay una estufa con horno en tu dormitorio? _____

7. ¿Hay un microondas en tu casa? _____

8. ¿Hay un televisor en el dormitorio de tu hermano o hermana? _____

9. ¿Hay una alfombra en la sala? _____

10. ¿De qué color es la alfombra? _____

Yo practico

A. A new appliance store has just opened. Your mother wants to know what they have on display. Look at the store window and name all the things you see.

_____

_____

_____

_____

_____

_____

_____

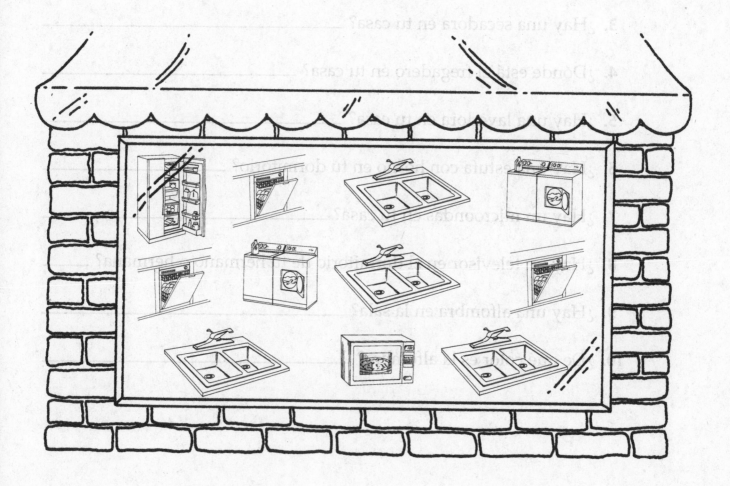

_____

_____

_____

B. Things are happening all around the house! Read the sentences and say the name of the appliance you need to help you with each problem.

1. Memo fell down in the mud and his clothes are a mess! What does he

   need? _____

2. The turkey is stuffed and ready to be cooked. Where does it go?

   _____

3. The birthday party is over. Now there are sixteen plates of pizza and

   cake crumbs. Where should they go? _____

4. The ham will spoil if it's left out. Where should it go?

   _____

5. Señor Méndez fell into the swimming pool. Now his clothing is

   soaking wet. What does he need? _____

6. Ana María has no time to cook dinner tonight but she still has the
   leftovers from last night's delicious rice with chicken and black bean
   soup she ordered from a Mexican restaurant. What does she need?

   _____

7. The eggs and the vegetables are ready to be mixed to cook a yummy

   omelet. Where do you cook them? _____

Yo imagino

The movers did a terrible job moving your family's things into your new house! Nothing is where it should be. Draw a picture of your mixed-up house. Then say at least five sentences to describe it.

Lección **8**

¡Vamos a jugar en la casa!

Yo aprendo el vocabulario

la televisión	el radio	el cartel
los carritos	la muñeca	los juguetes
el disco compacto	el lector de discos compactos	

Más vocabulario

Veo _____.

Escucho música en _____.

Juego con _____.

¿Qué quieres hacer?

Quiero (ver, escuchar, jugar con) _____.

Yo hablo

Your aunt from out of town is visiting your family. She wants to know what you do for fun. Listen to her questions. Then take turns answering.

1. ¿Qué haces con la televisión? _____

2. ¿Qué haces con el radio? _____

3. ¿Tienes muchos carteles en tu dormitorio? _____

4. ¿Hay carteles en tu salón de clases? _____

5. ¿Juegas con carritos? _____

6. ¿Cuántos carritos tienes? _____

7. ¿Juegas con muñecas? _____

8. ¿Cuántas muñecas tienes? _____

9. ¿En qué escuchas música? _____

10. ¿Tienes muchos discos compactos? _____

Yo practico

A reporter is doing a survey in a toy store to find out what children like to do. How do the children answer his question? Look at the pictures and say what each child says to the reporter. Begin your sentences with **Anabel (Gloria, Federico, Marcia, Adán, Ariel) dice «_____».**

Anabel

Gloria

Federico

Adán

Ariel

Marcia

Anabel dice _____

Gloria dice _____

Federico dice _____

Adán dice _____

Ariel dice _____

Marcia dice _____

Yo juego

It's a rainy afternoon, but Sonia and her friends are happy to play at her house. Help Sonia and her friends find their things. Draw a line from each child to the object he or she wants. Then say a sentence about what each child wants. Begin your sentences by saying **Quiero (ver, escuchar, jugar con)** _____.

Yo imagino

Plan your at-home activities for a whole week. Draw a toy or a home entertainment appliance for each day of the week and say what you want to do that day. Then choose a classmate and ask him or her what he or she wants to do each day of the week.

lunes	martes
miércoles	jueves
viernes	sábado
domingo	

Lección 9
Vamos a contar hasta setenta

Yo aprendo el vocabulario

sesenta y uno	61
sesenta y dos	62
sesenta y tres	63
sesenta y cuatro	64
sesenta y cinco	65
sesenta y seis	66
sesenta y siete	67
sesenta y ocho	68
sesenta y nueve	69
setenta	70

Más vocabulario

¿Cuánto es _____ menos _____?

Es/Son _____.

Yo hablo

Solve and then read aloud the following addition and subtraction problems.

1. 51 + 10 = __61__   sesenta uno

2. 69 – 7 = __62__   sisenta y dose

3. 70 – 5 = __65__   sisenta y cinco

4. 60 + 7 = __67__   sisenta y seite

5. 62 + 8 = __70__   sisenta y cincuenta y ocho

6. 59 + 9 = __58__   sisenta y tres e

7. 70 – 7 = __63__

8. 68 – 4 = __64__   sisenta y catro

9. 53 + 13 = __40__   caurenta

10. 70 – 1 = __69__   sisesenta y nueve

Yo practico

These lucky people have the winning tickets in the school raffle. They don't know yet which prizes they have won. Look at each person's number. Then find the prize that also has that number. Finally, say the number and the prize the person has won.

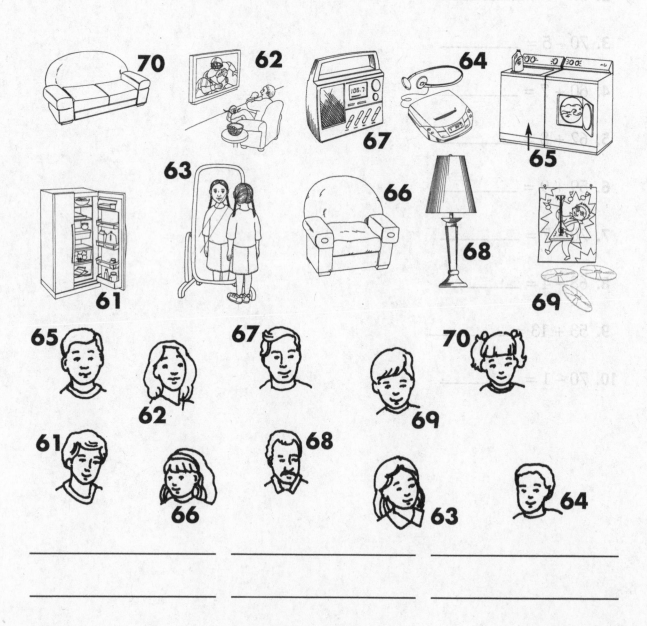

_____ _____ _____

_____ _____ _____

_____ _____ _____

_____

Yo juego

A. As you already know, at the Annual Artist Alphabet contest, each artist must draw a picture only of things that start with the letter on his or her easel. This year, you can choose any letter between *a* and *z* and write it on the easel. Then draw pictures of objects or write numbers from 0 to 70 that start with this letter. Take turns with your classmates to point to the objects you drew and say their names.

B. Take a survey to find out what your classmates want to do in their spare time today. Assign a number between 61 and 70 to each of eight of your classmates. Then ask them what they want to do, based on the items pictured below. As each of them answers, draw a line between his or her number and the item they want to do. Last, read aloud the results of your survey for the rest of the class. You may also ask family members, neighbors, and teachers.

Lección 10

¿Qué podemos hacer durante el invierno?

Yo aprendo el vocabulario

esquiar	patinar	hacer gimnasia
pescar	el invierno	la primavera
el verano	el otoño	

Yo hablo

A child from Argentina wants to know about the seasons in the United States. Listen to the questions. Then take turns with your classmates to answer them.

1. ¿Qué quieres hacer en primavera? _____

2. ¿Cuáles son los meses de la primavera? _____

3. ¿Qué quieres hacer en verano? _____

4. ¿Cuáles son los meses del verano? _____

5. ¿Qué quieres hacer en otoño? _____

6. ¿Cuáles son los meses del otoño? _____

7. ¿Qué quieres hacer en invierno? _____

8. ¿Cuáles son los meses del invierno? _____

9. ¿Qué deportes practicas? _____

10. ¿Qué mes es tu mes favorito? _____

Yo practico

A. A survey is being taken in your school to find out what children like to do at different times of the year. How would you answer? Listen to the questions. After each question, look at the four pictures in each row and circle two: one picture for the season of the year the person who is taking the survey asks you about, and one picture for the activity you like to do during that particular season. Finally, say in a complete sentence what you like to do and when.

1. ¿Qué quieres hacer en invierno?

_____

2. ¿Qué quieres hacer en verano?

_____

3. ¿Qué quieres hacer en primavera?

_____

4. ¿Qué quieres hacer en otoño?

_____

5. ¿Qué más quieres hacer en invierno?

_____

6. ¿Qué más quieres hacer en verano?

_____

B. Does each season make you think of certain sports or activities? In each box below, draw three or four activities that go with the season. Then, say aloud the names of the sports or activities you drew.

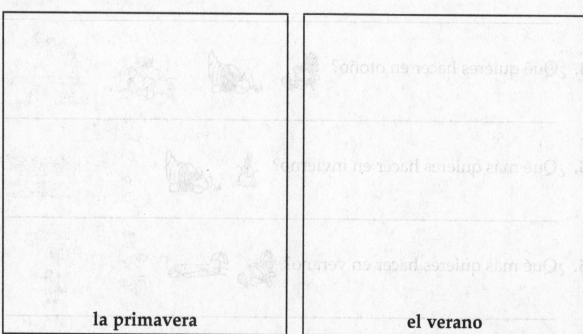

el invierno	**el otoño**
la primavera	**el verano**

Yo juego

Ask ten people when their birthdays are. Using numbers, write each date in the shape for the season that the date falls in. Remember to write the number of the day of the month first and then the number of the month. Compare your finding with your classmates. Which season has the most birthdays? Which month has the most birthdays?

Example: **28/8 (Rita)**

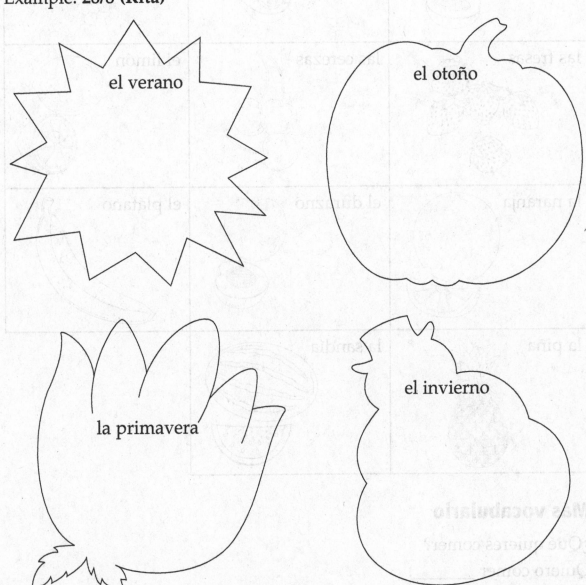

el verano

el otoño

la primavera

el invierno

Lección 11

¿Qué quieres comer?

Yo aprendo el vocabulario

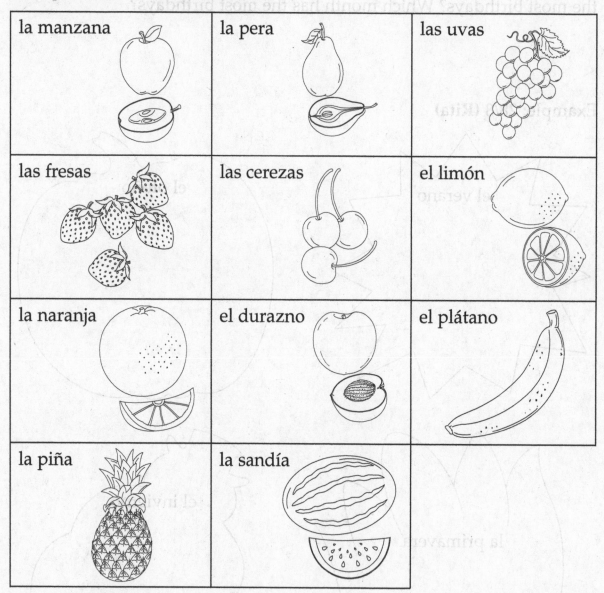

la manzana	la pera	las uvas
las fresas	las cerezas	el limón
la naranja	el durazno	el plátano
la piña	la sandía	

Más vocabulario

¿Qué quieres comer?

Quiero comer _____.

Yo practico

A. Color one box on the left red, one yellow, one orange, one purple, and one green. Draw a line connecting each colored box to the fruit of that color. Then write the name of the fruit next to its picture.

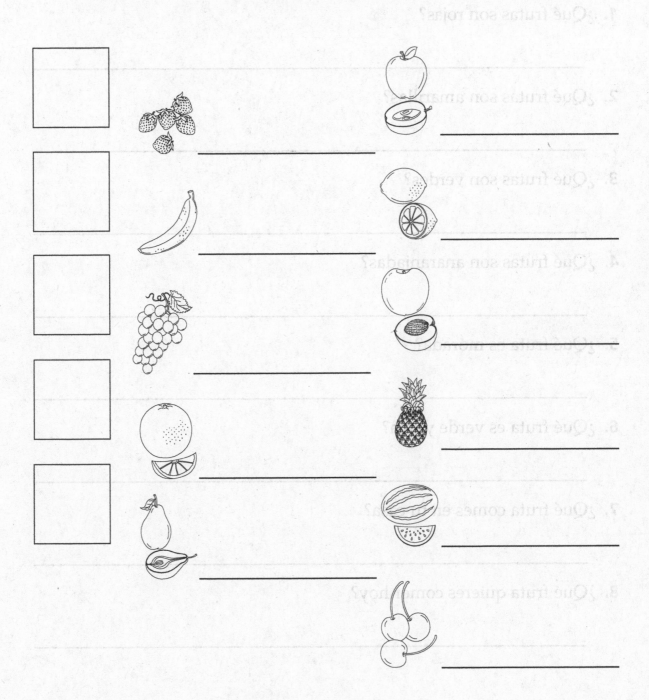

B. Your sister starts her new job at the supermarket tomorrow. They will be testing her on what she knows about fruits. Listen to the questions and help her prepare. Take turns saying the answers. You can also draw your answers in the space provided.

1. ¿Qué frutas son rojas?

_____

2. ¿Qué frutas son amarillas?

_____

3. ¿Qué frutas son verdes?

_____

4. ¿Qué frutas son anaranjadas?

_____

5. ¿Qué fruta es morada?

_____

6. ¿Qué fruta es verde y roja?

_____

7. ¿Qué fruta comes en tu casa?

_____

8. ¿Qué fruta quieres comer hoy?

_____

C. It is almost time for a snack and the children in señor Riera's class are thinking of their favorite fruit. Señor Riera wants to know what each child wants to eat. Listen to his questions and look at the picture. Then say each child's answer.

Yo imagino

Did you know that you can find some fruits only at certain times of the year? On a separate sheet of paper, draw and color some fruits that you can find in each season. Cut out your drawings and glue them inside the circle showing the season in which they belong.

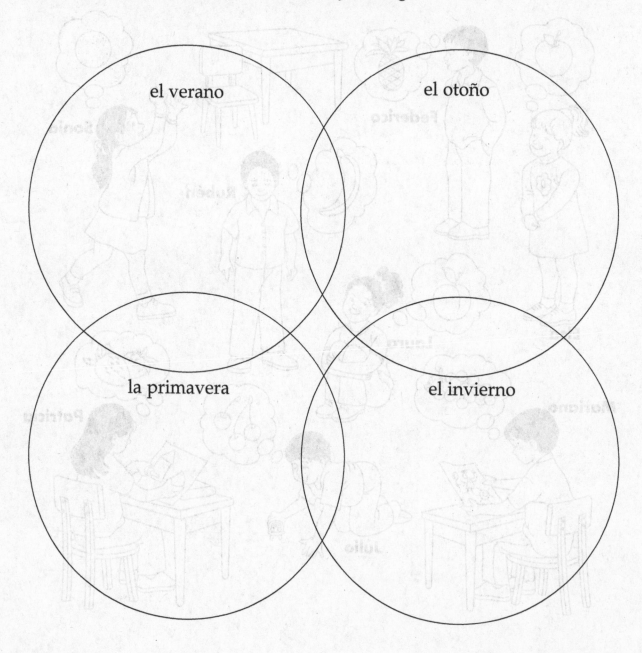

el verano

el otoño

la primavera

el invierno

Lección 12

¿Cuándo comemos?

Yo aprendo el vocabulario

el desayuno	el almuerzo	la cena
el tenedor	la cuchara	el cuchillo
la servilleta	la taza	el vaso

el plato	**Más vocabulario**
	¿Cuándo comes _____?
	Como _____ por _____.

Yo hablo

You are staying at a hotel for a weekend. The hostess wants to know when you eat each meal so she can have your meals prepared for you. Listen to the questions. Then take turns answering them.

1. ¿Cuándo comes el desayuno? _____

2. ¿Cuándo comes el almuerzo? _____

3. ¿Cuándo comes la cena? _____

4. ¿Cuándo comes naranjas (plátanos, manzanas, fresas, etc.)? _____

Yo practico

A. This is the first time Pedrito has eaten in a restaurant. He has many questions to ask his mother. What does she answer? Listen to Pedrito's questions, look at the pictures, and say your answers.

1. _____

2.  _____

3. _____

4. _____

5.  _____

6.  _____

7.  _____

B. Pedrito is still not sure what to do. He wants to know what to use to eat or drink these foods or beverages. Look at the pictures and draw what you would use to eat or drink each item in the space provided. Then take turns calling out the name of the tableware you would use to eat or drink each item.

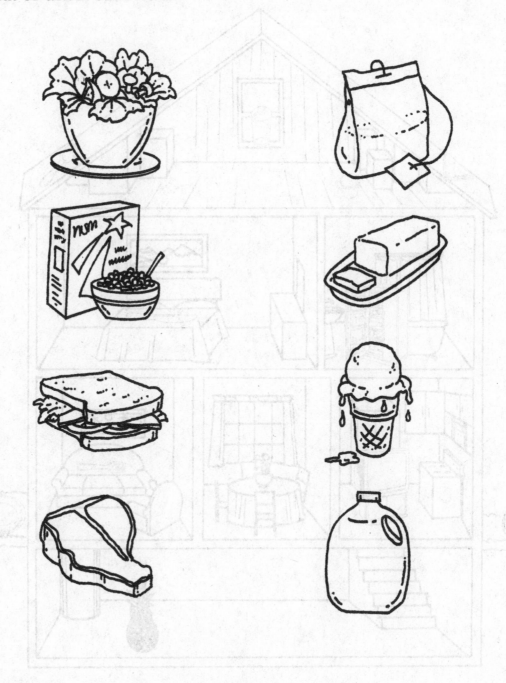

Yo juego

Everyone loves silly Uncle Serafín's visits, but he is so messy! Find and circle eleven things left in the wrong places in the house below. Then take turns saying a short sentence about each item.

Yo imagino

Plan a surprise **fiesta de cumpleaños** for a friend or a family member. Make your shopping list here before you go to the store by drawing and coloring items in the space below. What will you need to set the table? What colors would your friends or family like? How many people will you invite? Don't forget to pick up some fruit for the party!

Now that you have bought your supplies, set the table. On a separate sheet of paper, draw a picture of the table, set and ready for a surprise **fiesta de cumpleaños.**

Lección 13

¿Qué te gusta?

Yo aprendo el vocabulario

la leche	el cereal	el pan tostado	el jugo (de ____)
la sopa	las galletas	el queso	el sándwich
la carne	la papa	el pescado	las zanahorias
el pollo	el arroz	la lechuga	el tomate

Más vocabulario

¡Qué rico!

¿Qué te gusta?

Me gusta _____.

No me gusta _____.

No me gustan _____.

¿Te gusta _____?

Sí, me gusta.

No, no me gusta.

¿Te gustan _____?

Sí, me gustan.

No, no me gustan.

Yo practico

Elena and Pilar are walking home from school. They are very hungry
and all they can think about is food! Listen to Elena's questions. Then
look at the pictures to decide how Pilar will answer. Say the answers.

1. ¿Te gustan las papas? _____

2. ¿Te gustan las zanahorias? _____

3. ¿Te gusta la sopa con galletas? _____

4. ¿Te gusta el jugo de frutas? _____

5. ¿Te gusta el sándwich? _____

6. ¿Te gusta el arroz? _____

7. ¿Te gusta el cereal? _____

8. ¿Te gusta la leche? _____

9. ¿Te gustan las manzanas? _____

10. ¿Te gusta el pollo? _____

11. ¿Te gustan las naranjas? _____

12. ¿Te gusta la sandía? _____

Yo juego

What if you went to a cafeteria for a meal and were all ready to pick out your food, but you were blindfolded? What kind of meal would you end up with? Close your eyes and turn the workbook around a few times, point to a food and open your eyes. Name the food to which you are pointing. Then circle or color in the picture on this page. Choose four more foods the same way. Who in your class has the most unusual meal?

Yo imagino

A. Look at the pictures below and ask your classmates silly questions about each pair.

1.	5.	9.
2.	6.	10.
3.	7.	11.
4.	8.	12.

B. The school cafeteria is looking for new meals to serve. Draw and color a picture of your favorite meal on this plate. Share it with your class.

Lección 14

Vamos a practicar lo que hemos aprendido

Yo practico

Listen to the sentences and circle the two pictures that you hear in each sentence.

1. En invierno quiero esquiar y patinar.

2. En primavera quiero jugar al béisbol y andar en bicicleta.

3. En verano quiero ir de picnic y nadar.

4. En otoño quiero jugar al baloncesto y jugar al fútbol americano.

Yo juego

The Ritz Hotel makes a picture book out of the daily menu, and guests must circle the food they want to order. First, circle the items you would like to order for breakfast, lunch, and dinner. Then choose a partner as a waiter or waitress, and have him or her tell you the names of the food you have circled.

El menú del Ritz

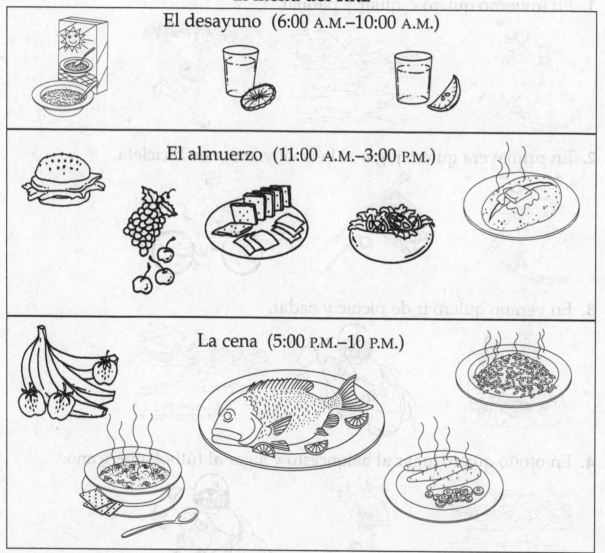

El desayuno (6:00 A.M.–10:00 A.M.)

El almuerzo (11:00 A.M.–3:00 P.M.)

La cena (5:00 P.M.–10 P.M.)

Yo imagino

Mimi and Melinda's room is a mess! Circle the objects that do not belong in the bedroom. Then tell the girls where to put everything. For example say, **Pon la bicicleta en el garaje.**

OCTUBRE

Yo juego

Play a game. Flip a coin to determine whether you move one space or two. If it lands on heads, move two spaces. If it lands on tails, move one space. When you land on a space, you must say the letter or number correctly in Spanish. If you answer incorrectly, you lose a turn. The first player to the end wins!

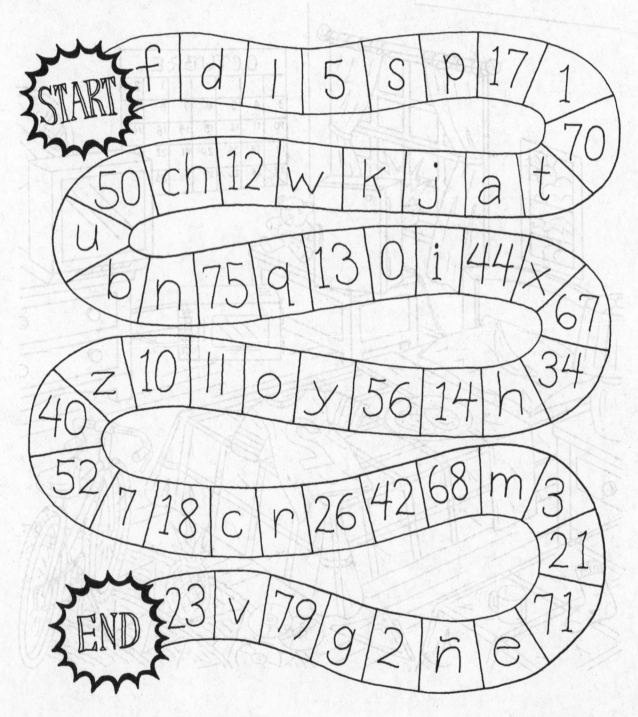

Yo practico

Match the words on the left with the pictures on the right. Draw a line to connect them.

1. la casa

2. el sillón

3. el radio

4. el televisor

5. la manzana

6. el limón

7. el tenedor

8. el sofá

9. la taza

10. el vaso

11. el disco compacto

12. la sopa

13. el garaje

14. el sándwich

15. las uvas

Lección 15

Vamos a contar hasta ochenta

Yo aprendo el vocabulario

setenta y uno	71
setenta y dos	72
setenta y tres	73
setenta y cuatro	74
setenta y cinco	75
setenta y seis	76
setenta y siete	77
setenta y ocho	78
setenta y nueve	79
ochenta	80

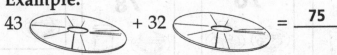

Yo hablo

Complete the following addition and subtraction problems. Write the result using numbers. Then read the problems aloud for the class. The first one is done for you.

1. Example:

43 [CD] + 32 [CD] = **75** [CD]

2. 50 [truck] + 28 [truck] = _____ [truck]

3. 25 [doll] + 30 [doll] + 25 [doll] = _____ [doll]

4. 79 [picture] – 7 [picture] = _____ [picture]

5. 80 [apple] – 4 [apple] = _____ [apple]

6. 77 [banana] – 20 [banana] – 10 [banana] = _____ [banana]

7. 37 [glass] + 36 [glass] = _____ [glass]

8. 49 [triangle] + 31 [triangle] – 1 [triangle] = _____ [triangle]

Yo practico

The Herreras are ordering their food by the numbers on the menu. What does each person want to eat? First, read the number each person is thinking of. Then find that number on the menu and say what the person wants to eat. For example, you may say, **Carmen quiere comer el setenta y nueve. Ella quiere comer el plátano y la naranja.**

Yo juego

Fefi and Mimo, the Morelos family's cats, are on the roof when they hear Catalina Morelos calling them. They race down through the house, but who will arrive first? Play this game with a partner. One partner follows Fefi's path and one follows Mimo's path. Take turns saying the numbers in your path aloud. If you say the wrong number, you must stay on that number until you say it correctly. If you say the correct number, you may go to the next one.

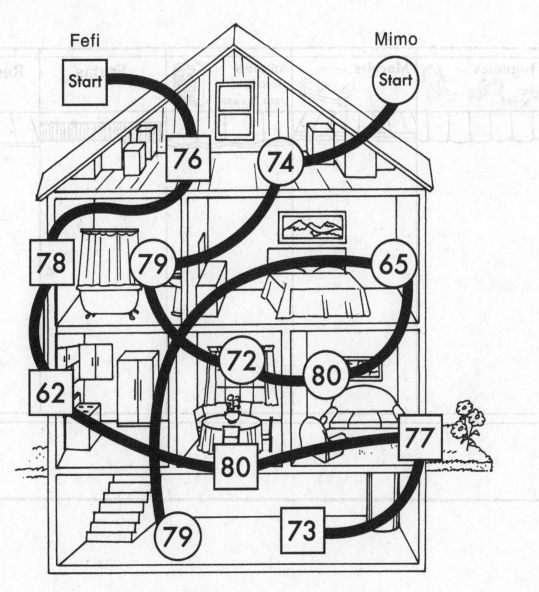

Yo imagino

You are visiting a new town with your mother. What do you think is
sold in each of these stores? Name five items for each store and draw
them in the store windows.

Juguetes	Muebles	Aparatos eléctricos para la casa	Frutas	Restaurante

Lección 16

¿Qué aprendemos en la escuela?

Yo aprendo el vocabulario

la clase de _____

las ciencias	el arte	las matemáticas
las computadoras	la música	los estudios sociales
el inglés	el español	la hora de recreo
la educación física		

Más vocabulario

¿Qué haces en (la clase de) _____?

Estudio.

Pinto.

Dibujo.

Leo.

Canto.

Hago ejercicios.

Yo hablo

It is the first time you have seen your grandmother since starting school this year. She has a lot of questions for you. Take turns answering her questions.

1. ¿Qué clases tienes en la escuela? _____

2. ¿Te gusta la clase de matemáticas? _____

3. ¿Te gusta la clase de español? _____

4. ¿Tienes un libro de estudios sociales? _____

5. ¿Te gusta la clase de arte? _____

6. ¿Qué haces en la clase de arte? _____

7. ¿Qué haces en la clase de ciencias? _____

8. ¿Qué haces en la clase de música? _____

9. ¿Qué haces en la clase de computadoras? _____

10. ¿Qué clase es tu clase favorita? _____

11. ¿Qué clase no te gusta? _____

12. ¿Haces ejercicios en la clase de computadoras? _____

Yo practico

Adela has been getting out all the things she will need for school today. Her little brother Paquito wants to know what class each item is for. Look at the pictures and name the class in which you would use each object.

1.

6.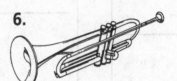

2.

7.

3.

8.
niño

4.

9.

5. $\begin{array}{r} 22 \\ + 44 \\ \hline 66 \end{array}$

10.
boy

Yo juego

Señora Orellano is teasing her class this morning. She tells the children the plans for the day, but mixes up the important words. Can you fix the mixed-up words?

1. als taimácsmeta

_____

2. le ruzoelma

_____

3. el snégli

_____

4. sal pacomtudraso

_____

5. le trae

_____

6. slo esdiostu cialsoes

_____

7. al hoar eld recoer

_____

8. le elpñosa

_____

9. al icúsam

_____

10. sal encicias

_____

11. al caciónedu cafísi

_____

Yo practico

The teachers love all of the school subjects! What are your favorites? Draw two lists below—one to show your favorite school subjects, and another to show your least favorite subjects. Try to include at least four drawings in each list and don't forget about lunchtime. Write your name on top of the sheet of paper. Trade lists with your classmates and take turns reading them aloud.

Lección 17

Vamos al zoológico

Yo aprendo el vocabulario

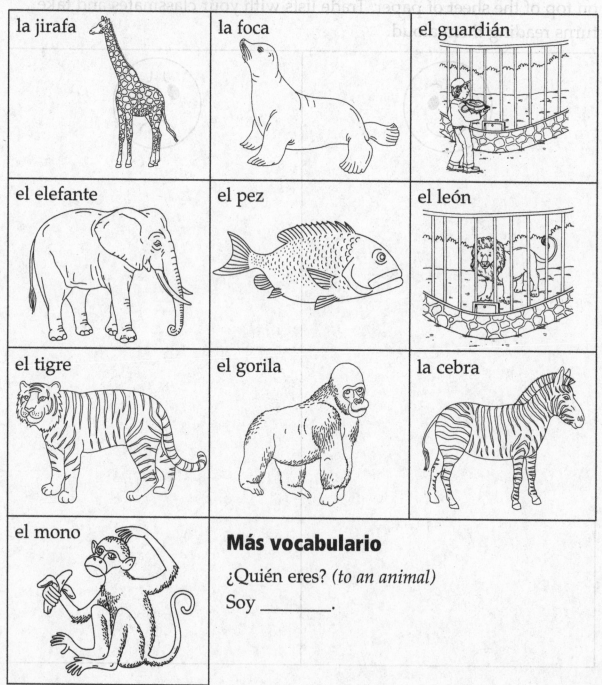

la jirafa

la foca

el guardián

el elefante

el pez

el león

el tigre

el gorila

la cebra

el mono

Más vocabulario

¿Quién eres? (to an animal)

Soy _____.

Yo hablo

Your friend Natán is curious about all the animals at the zoo. Look at the pictures of the zoo animals and listen to his questions. Pretend you are **el guardián** and answer his questions with what you know about each animal.

1. ¿Quién eres? ¿Te gusta nadar?

2. ¿Quién eres? ¿Te gusta comer plátanos?

3. ¿Quién eres? ¿Te gusta nadar?

4. ¿Quién eres? ¿Te gusta cantar?

5. ¿Quién eres? ¿Te gusta comer pan tostado?

6. ¿Quién eres? ¿Te gusta cantar?

7. ¿Quién eres? ¿Tienes hambre?

8. ¿Quién eres? ¿Cómo eres?

Yo practico

The zookeeper feels like being silly. He has decided to speak in riddles today. Listen to the riddles and figure out who or what he is talking about.

1. Tengo una cara fea. Soy negro. Me gusta comer plátanos.

2. Soy muy grande. Tengo orejas muy grandes. Soy gris.

3. Soy marrón. Como plátanos. Vivo en los árboles.

4. Me gusta el agua. Como muchos peces. Me gusta jugar.

5. Soy anaranjado y negro. Soy un gato grande. Como animales pequeños.

6. Soy un gato grande. Tengo mucho pelo. Me gusta comer la carne.

7. Soy blanca y negra. Me gusta correr. El caballo es mi hermano.

8. Soy muy alta. Soy muy bonita. Tengo miedo del león.

9. Estoy en el zoológico todos los días. No soy un animal. No tengo miedo de los animales.

Yo juego

Say the name that goes with each picture below. Complete the crossword puzzle by filling in the missing letters.

Yo imagino

A. These strange-looking animals are mixtures of two animals! Figure out which two animals are in each mixture and take turns with the rest of the class to name them.

B. Draw two of your own "mixed-up" animals in the space below. Share them with your class. Take turns with your classmates to figure out which two animals are in each mixture.

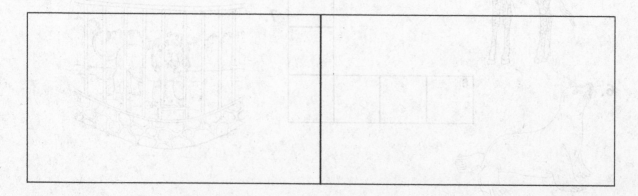

Lección 18

¿Cómo son los animales del zoológico?

Yo aprendo el vocabulario

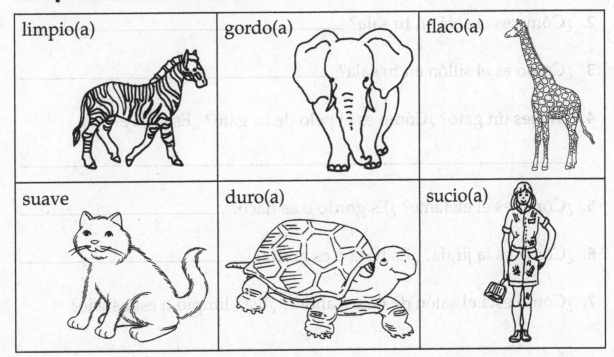

limpio(a)	gordo(a)	flaco(a)
suave	duro(a)	sucio(a)

Más vocabulario

¿Cómo es?

Es _____.

No es ____.

¿Está _____?

Sí, está _____.

No, no está ____.

Yo hablo

Everyone has a lot of questions for you today! Listen to the questions and take turns answering them.

1. ¿Cómo es tu silla en el salón de clases? _____

2. ¿Cómo es el sofá en tu sala? _____

3. ¿Cómo es el sillón en tu sala? _____

4. ¿Tienes un gato? ¿Cómo es el pelo de tu gato? ¿Es suave?

_____

5. ¿Cómo es el elefante? ¿Es gordo o es flaco? _____

6. ¿Cómo es la jirafa? ¿Es flaca o es gorda? _____

7. ¿Cómo está el salón de clases ahora? ¿Está limpio o está sucio?

_____

8. ¿Cómo están tus zapatos ahora? ¿Están sucios o están limpios?

_____

9. Pongo los platos en el lavaplatos. ¿Cómo están los platos?

_____

Yo practico

Look at the zookeeper and all of the animals in the zoo. How would you describe them? Choose an adjective to describe each animal (and the zookeeper!) to the class. For example you might say, **El pájaro es bonito.**

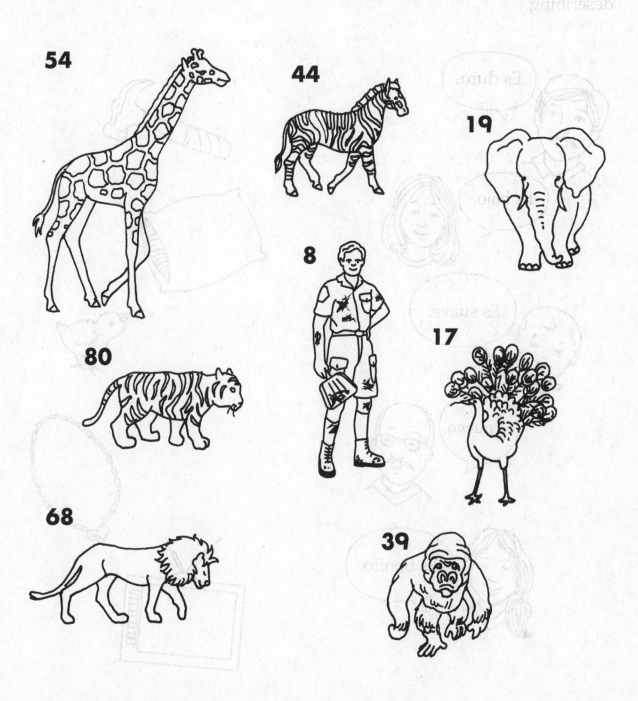

54

44

19

80

8

17

68

39

Yo juego

The Aguilera family is playing a favorite after-dinner game. Each person describes something nearby. The others have to guess what it is. You can play it, too. Draw a line from each person to the object he or she is describing.

Yo imagino

Create your own zoo! As you draw and color the animals in your zoo, think of all the adjectives you have learned. You may want to keep in mind one or more adjectives as you draw a particular animal. Show your zoo to your classmates and describe it. You can say things like, **"La jirafa es alta y bonita. El elefante es grande, gordo y gris."**

Lección 19

¿En qué edificio vives?

Yo aprendo el vocabulario

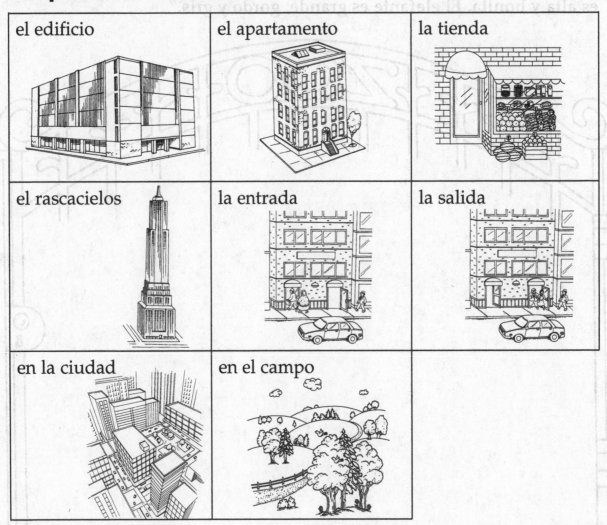

el edificio	el apartamento	la tienda
el rascacielos	la entrada	la salida
en la ciudad	en el campo	

Más vocabulario

cerca de

lejos de

delante de

detrás de

¿En qué edificio vives?

Vivo en _____.

No vivo en _____.

Yo hablo

Laura has just moved into town. She asks her new neighbor Sonia lots of questions about her new street. What does Sonia say? Look at the pictures to answer Laura's questions.

1. ¿Qué es? _____

2. ¿Qué es? _____

3. ¿Qué es? _____

4. ¿Qué es? _____

5. ¿Qué es? _____

Yo practico

Óscar has just moved to a new city. His friend Tina wants to know where everything is in his new city. Listen to Tina's questions. Then look at the map and help Óscar answer them.

Yo juego

These children came with their parents to town and got lost. They can describe the buildings their parents are in, but they don't know how to go there. The policeman wants to take each child to his or her parents by the shortest way possible. Read each child's description. Then, on the next page, draw a line from the police station to the building each child is describing. Use a different color for each path, and always find the shortest way.

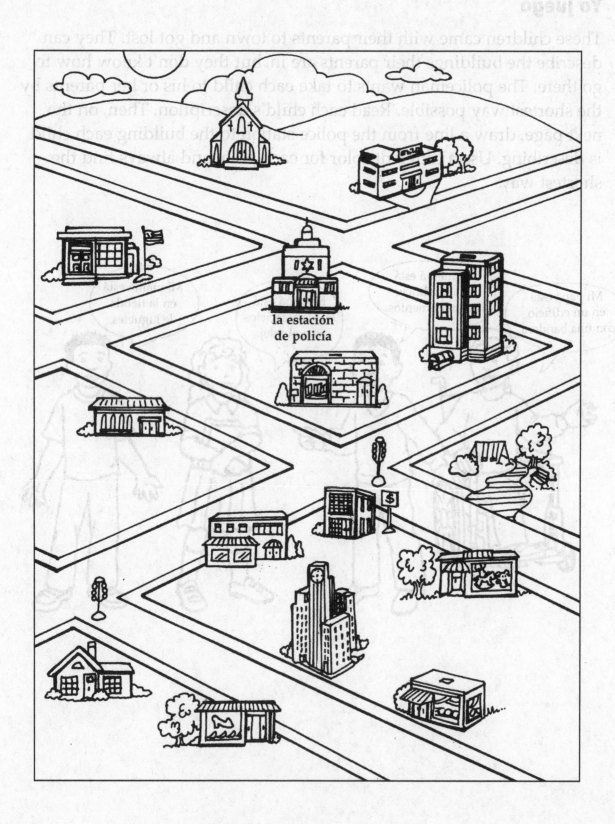

la estación
de policía

Yo imagino

Draw the buildings on a street in a large city. Give them windows, doors, entrances, exits, gardens, garages, and anything else you can think of. Name your street. Try to sell someone a house or building on the street. Tell the person how wonderful everything is (for example, **"Los apartamentos son grandes, bonitos y limpios."**).

Lección 20

Vamos a contar hasta noventa

Yo aprendo el vocabulario

ochenta y uno	81
ochenta y dos	82
ochenta y tres	83
ochenta y cuatro	84
ochenta y cinco	85
ochenta y seis	86
ochenta y siete	87
ochenta y ocho	88
ochenta y nueve	89
noventa	90

Yo hablo

A friend from another country has a lot of questions for you. Listen to the questions, then take turns answering them.

1. ¿Qué quieres hacer el sábado? _____

2. ¿Qué te gusta hacer con tu familia? _____

3. ¿Qué quieres hacer en primavera? _____

4. ¿Qué quieres comer para la cena hoy? _____

5. ¿Qué te gusta comer en la cafetería de la escuela? _____

6. ¿Qué te gusta comer para el desayuno? _____

7. ¿Cuándo comes el desayuno? _____

8. ¿Qué fruta es tu fruta favorita? _____

9. ¿Hay un restaurante cerca de tu casa? ¿Qué comes en el restaurante?

_____

Yo practico

Lisa has drawn a neighborhood of toy houses with numbers by the houses. Now she wants to put some silly decorations on the houses. Listen to the instructions and draw the objects on the houses.

- Dibuja la taza en el número ochenta y dos.

- Dibuja el vaso en el número ochenta y ocho.

- Dibuja el carrito en el número noventa.

- Dibuja el gato en el número ochenta y tres.

- Dibuja la cuchara en el número ochenta y siete.

- Dibuja el tenedor en el número ochenta y nueve.

- Dibuja las ventanas en el número ochenta y uno.

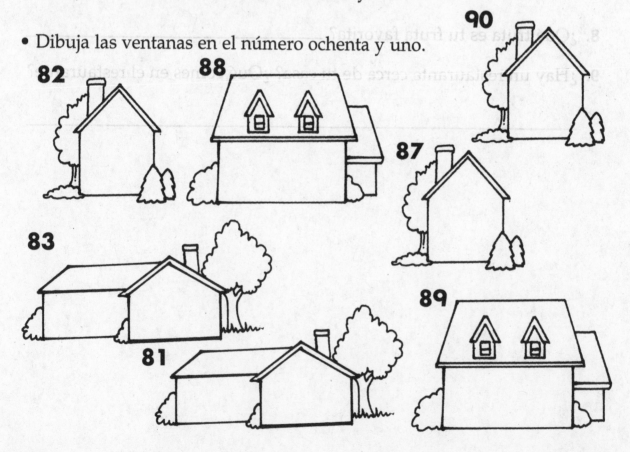

Yo juego

Play this game with a partner. Pretend that you and your partner are taking a walk in a strange town. As you walk, you see many unusual things. Call out a number. Your partner must describe whatever is next to the number (for example, if you say **ochenta y uno,** your partner would say **El sillón es suave.**). Then it's your partner's turn to call out a number and you must describe what you see next to the number.

Yo imagino

Here are some empty stores. It's up to you to bring them to life. Decide which one will be **la tienda de frutas, la tienda de juguetes, la tienda de música,** and **la tienda de muebles** (the furniture store). Give each shop an address between 81 and 90, and a sign. Draw some items in each store. Share your picture with your class.

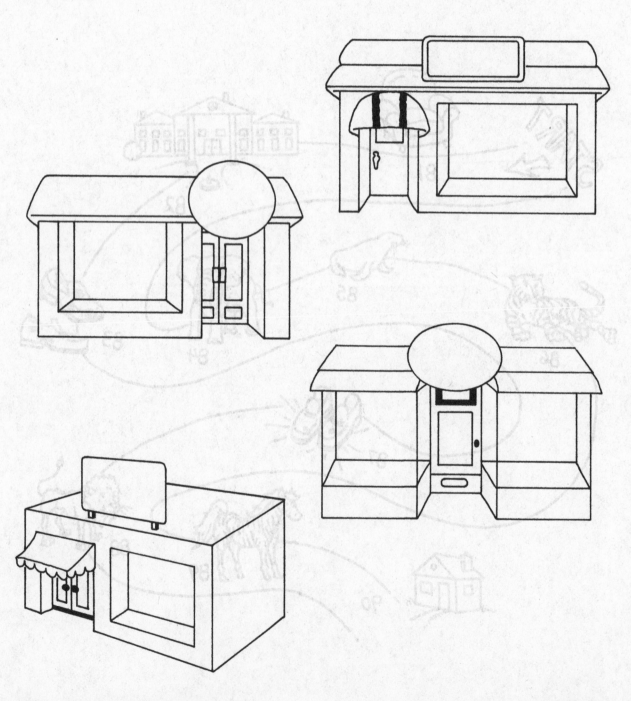

Lección 21

Vamos a lugares en nuestra ciudad

Yo aprendo el vocabulario

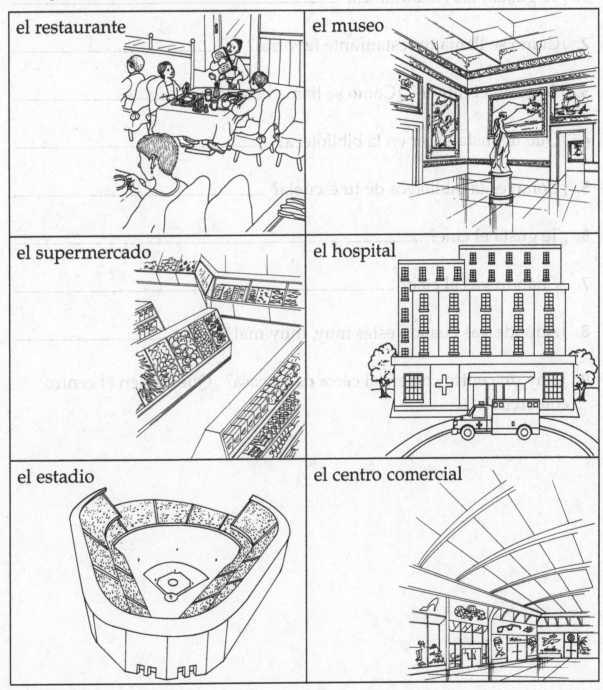

el restaurante

el museo

el supermercado

el hospital

el estadio

el centro comercial

Yo hablo

Your friend Tania is moving to your neighborhood with her mother. She wants to know about some of the stores and shops in the area. Listen to her questions. Then raise your hand and take turns answering them.

1. ¿Te gustan los restaurantes? _____

2. ¿Cómo se llama tu restaurante favorito? _____

3. ¿Te gusta el museo? ¿Cómo se llama el museo? _____

4. ¿Qué te gusta hacer en la biblioteca? _____

5. ¿Cómo es la biblioteca de tu escuela? _____

6. ¿Te gusta el cine? _____

7. ¿Cuándo vas al cine? _____

8. ¿Adónde vas cuando estás muy, muy mal? _____

9. ¿Hay un centro comercial cerca de tu casa? ¿Qué hay en el centro comercial?

_____

Yo practico

What would you do in these situations? Listen to the sentence. Then listen to the questions and look at the pictures. Circle the picture that is your answer. Then share your answer with the rest of the class.

1. ¡Tienes hambre!
   ¿Adónde vas? ¿Vas al o al  ?

2. ¡Tienes dolor!
   ¿Adónde vas? ¿Vas a la  o al  ?

3. Quieres leer libros.
   ¿Adónde vas? ¿Vas a la  o al  ?

4. Quieres ver el arte.
   ¿Adónde vas? ¿Vas al  o al  ?

5. Quieres jugar al béisbol.
   ¿Adónde vas? ¿Vas al  o al  ?

6. Quieres ver los animales.
   ¿Adónde vas? ¿Vas al o al ?

7. Quieres ver los juguetes.
   ¿Adónde vas? ¿Vas al o a la ?

8. Quieres ver el juego de fútbol.
   ¿Adónde vas? ¿Vas al  o al ?

Yo juego

Play this game alone or with a friend. Below is a list of places you must go today. Flip a coin. If it shows "heads" move one space. If it shows "tails" move two spaces. The picture in each space should remind you where you must go. Say the name of the place out loud (for example, **"Voy al museo."**). If you can't remember, you miss your next turn. The first person to the end is the winner!

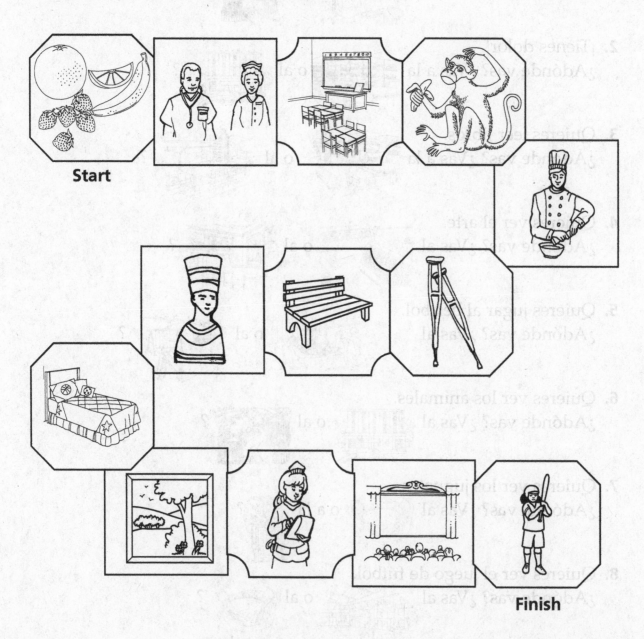

Start

Finish

Yo imagino

A. Have you ever wished you could plan everything you wanted to do for a whole week? Here is an empty calendar. Draw the activities and errands that you like to do. For instance, draw a library if you want to quietly read a book you don't have at home, or draw a baseball, a bat, or a glove (or the three of them!) if you want to play baseball. And if you really like something, do it a few times!

lunes	martes
miércoles	jueves

viernes	sábado	domingo

B. Lobo, **el perro,** wasn't feeling very good, so his owners took him to the vet. The vet took X-rays of his stomach. Imagine their surprise when they saw what he had eaten. He had swallowed one thing from each of the places listed below! Draw what might be in his stomach! Tell the vet what Lobo ate when you are asked.

el restaurante	el museo	el supermercado	el parque
el hospital	el estadio	el centro comercial	la biblioteca

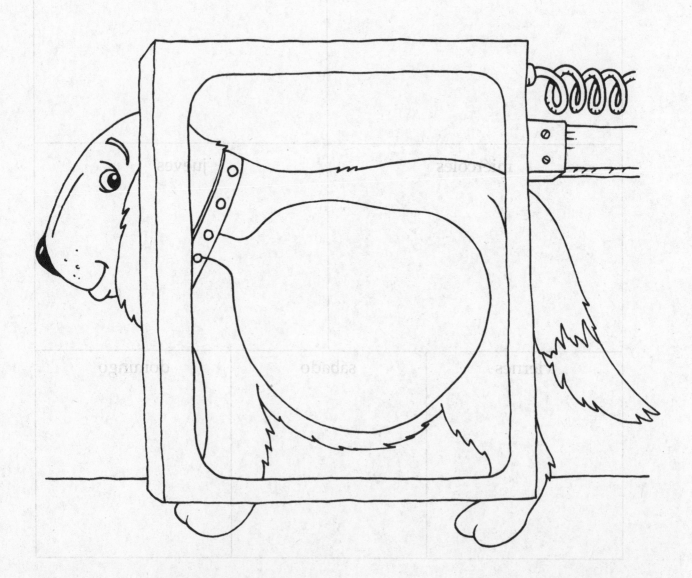

Lección 22

¿Dónde está la estación de trenes?

Yo aprendo el vocabulario

| la estación de trenes | el aeropuerto | la parada de autobús |
| el estacionamiento | la ciudad | el centro |

Yo hablo

Listen to the questions. Then raise your hand and take turns with your classmates to answer the questions.

1. ¿Cómo se llama tu ciudad? _____

2. ¿Qué hay en el centro de tu ciudad? _____

3. ¿Cómo vas al centro? _____

4. ¿Cómo vas a la escuela? _____

5. ¿Hay un estacionamiento grande en tu escuela? _____

6. ¿Adónde vas en el autobús? _____

7. ¿Está cerca o está lejos de tu casa la parada de autobús? _____

8. ¿Cuándo vas al aeropuerto? _____

Yo practico

It's Saturday morning and everyone in the city has someplace to go. Look at each picture. When you are called on, share with the rest of the class where you think the people are going and how they will get there.

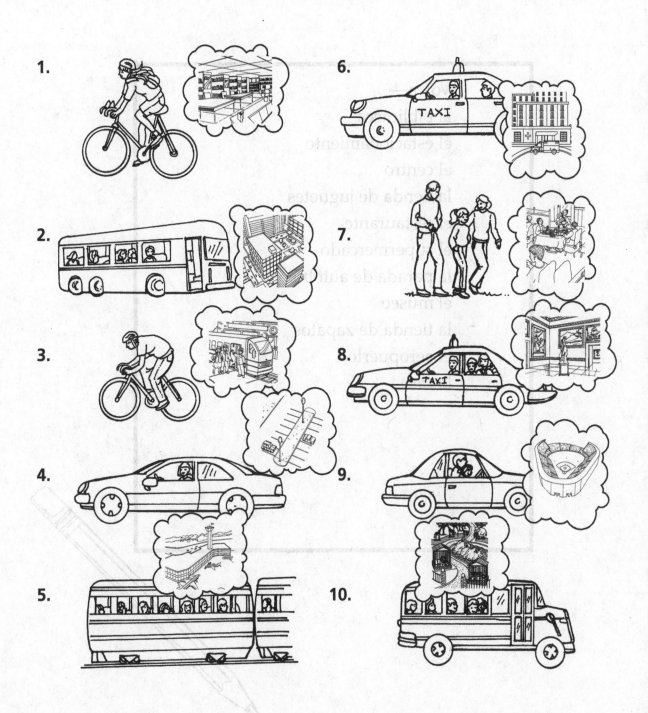

1.

2.

3.

4.

5.

6.

7.

8.

9.

10.

Yo juego

On the next page is a map of a little town. Listen to señora Romero's list of errands for the day. Help her do all her chores. Remember: She must do the errands in the order they are listed. Draw arrows through the streets to show the path you think she should take.

Voy a—
la biblioteca
el estacionamiento
el centro
la tienda de juguetes
el restaurante
el supermercado
la parada de autobús
el museo
la tienda de zapatos
el aeropuerto
la casa

Start Here

Yo imagino

Here is a story that you may make serious or silly. Listen to the first part of each sentence. Then choose a word from the three pictures to finish the sentence. Finally, share with the rest of the class your version of the story.

1. Hoy es sábado. Hace   .

2. Vivo en   .

3. Quiero comer el desayuno. Quiero comer   .

4. Ahora estoy muy bien. Voy al (a la)   .

5. En la calle, veo   .

6. Veo muchos carros y autobuses. Son muy   .

7. Voy al aeropuerto. Veo   .

8. Ahora tengo hambre. Voy al (a la)    .

9. Ahora tengo sueño. Voy al (a la)   .

Lección 23

Quiero tocar un instrumento

Yo aprendo el vocabulario

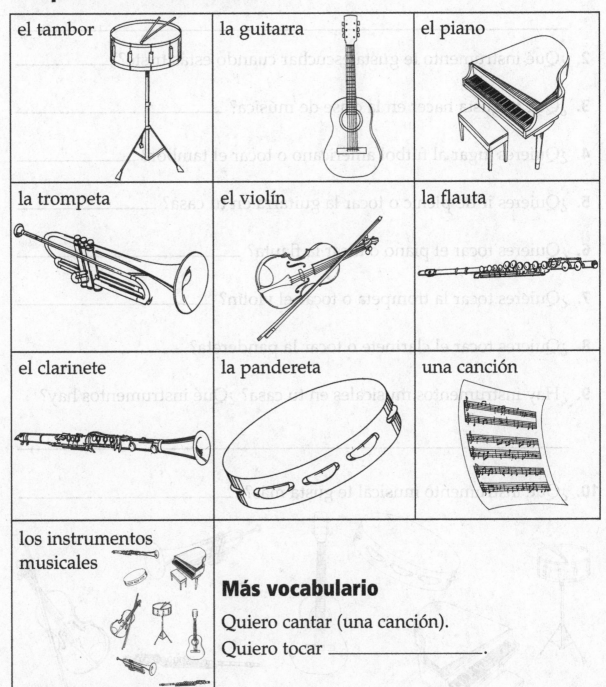

el tambor

la guitarra

el piano

la trompeta

el violín

la flauta

el clarinete

la pandereta

una canción

los instrumentos musicales

Más vocabulario

Quiero cantar (una canción).

Quiero tocar _____.

Yo hablo

Look at all the instruments! They are so beautiful it makes you want to play them all.

1. ¿Qué instrumento te gusta escuchar cuando estás contento (contenta)?

_____

2. ¿Qué instrumento te gusta escuchar cuando estás triste? _____

3. ¿Qué te gusta hacer en la clase de música? _____

4. ¿Quieres jugar al fútbol americano o tocar el tambor? _____

5. ¿Quieres ir de picnic o tocar la guitarra en tu casa? _____

6. ¿Quieres tocar el piano o tocar la flauta? _____

7. ¿Quieres tocar la trompeta o tocar el violín? _____

8. ¿Quieres tocar el clarinete o tocar la pandereta? _____

9. ¿Hay instrumentos musicales en tu casa? ¿Qué instrumentos hay?

_____

10. ¿Qué instrumento musical te gusta más? _____

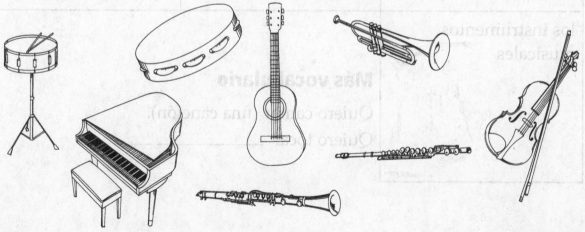

Yo practico

These people just heard a concert by the orchestra. Now they are all dreaming of becoming musicians. What does each person want to play? Look at the picture and say what musical instrument each person wants to play.

Yo juego

Look at the orchestra playing their . . . hey, wait a minute! Where are the instruments? Can you figure out what each musician is playing? Say the name of the missing instrument for each musician.

Yo imagino

Be a composer! Different kinds of music need different combinations of instruments. Draw the instruments you would use for each type of music. Then take turns with your classmates to name the instruments you drew. Finally, think of a catchy Spanish title for each song you plan to write and share your titles with the class.

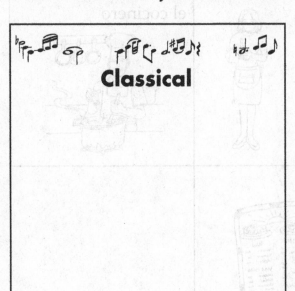

Classical

Rock

Country

Jazz

Lección 24

Vamos al restaurante

Yo aprendo el vocabulario

el camarero	la camarera	el cocinero
la cocinera	el menú	

Más vocabulario

¿Qué desea comer?

¿Qué desea beber?

Deseo _____.

No hay _____.

Yo hablo

The science class is taking a survey. They want to know what kinds of food you eat and drink and whether you like certain things. Listen to the questions. Then raise your hand and take turns answering them.

1. ¿Qué hay para comer en la cafetería de la escuela? _____

2. ¿Qué hay para comer en tu casa para el desayuno? _____

3. ¿Qué quieres comer hoy para el almuerzo? _____

4. ¿Qué quieres comer hoy para la cena? _____

5. ¿Hay frutas en la cocina de tu casa? _____

6. ¿Hay leche en el refrigerador de tu casa? _____

7. ¿Te gusta comer arroz con pollo? _____

8. ¿Hay sopa en la estufa de tu casa? _____

9. ¿Te gusta comer galletas y queso? _____

10. ¿Te gusta beber jugo de naranja? _____

Yo practico

The Méndez family is at a new restaurant and they don't have a menu yet. They are asking the waiter what the restaurant has. Look at the menu on this page and answer the questions for him.

Restaurante

Amalia

Sopas

sopa de pollo
sopa de papas

Bebidas

jugo de naranja
jugo de tomate
leche

Comidas

pescado
carne
pollo

Postres

plátanos
cerezas
fresas

arroz
papas

Yo juego

Five restaurant words and seven names of musical instruments are hidden in this puzzle. Find them and circle them. They go from left to right or from top to bottom. Take turns to share your findings with the rest of the class.

A	O	A	F	C	N	R	V	B	R	Y	P
R	É	I	L	S	M	V	B	F	A	L	A
C	A	M	A	R	E	R	O	Ú	R	I	N
A	E	S	U	P	N	L	C	L	I	C	D
M	I	N	T	A	Ú	P	I	A	N	O	E
A	C	L	A	R	I	N	E	T	E	C	R
R	C	A	O	E	T	J	O	A	Ú	I	E
E	E	V	I	O	L	Í	N	M	I	N	T
R	N	A	M	D	A	O	E	B	G	E	A
A	C	O	C	I	N	E	R	O	A	R	B
O	A	T	G	U	I	T	A	R	R	A	S

En el restaurante

camarero

camarera

menú

cocinero

cocinera

Instrumentos musicales

violín

tambor

piano

flauta

guitarra

clarinete

pandereta

Yo imagino

Very few people go to eat at the restaurant of señor Pepe Valenzuela. He is the **cocinero** and his wife, Carlota, is the **camarera.** Why is the restaurant empty? Just look at the menu, and you will see! Three dishes are already on the menu. Draw the basic ingredients of six more meals that you would never eat. Then share your not-so-delicious culinary creations with the rest of the class.

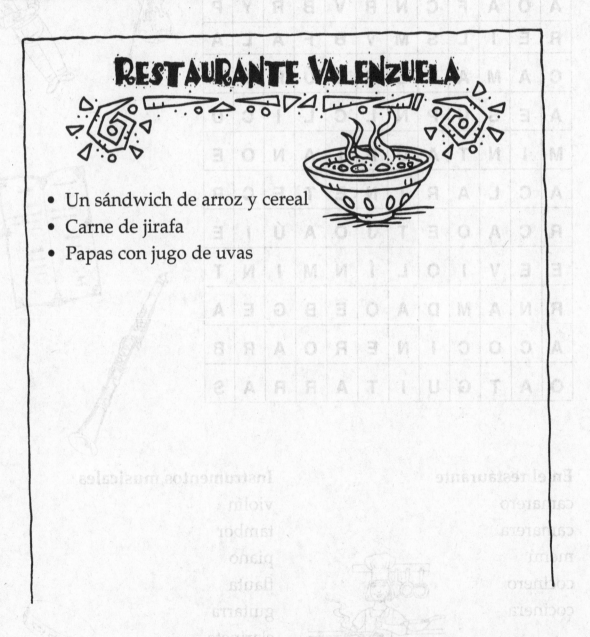

RESTAURANTE VALENZUELA

- Un sándwich de arroz y cereal
- Carne de jirafa
- Papas con jugo de uvas

Lección 25

Vamos a contar hasta cien

Yo aprendo el vocabulario

noventa y uno	91
noventa y dos	92
noventa y tres	93
noventa y cuatro	94
noventa y cinco	95
noventa y seis	96
noventa y siete	97
noventa y ocho	98
noventa y nueve	99
cien	100

Yo hablo

Your father is taking inventory at his hardware store. Some items come in packages of 2, 5, 10, 15, or 20. Help him count the total number.

1. Cuenta hasta cien de veinte en veinte (por ejemplo, 20, 40, etc.).

2. Cuenta hasta cien de diez en diez (por ejemplo, 10, 20, etc.).

3. Cuenta hasta cien de quince en quince (por ejemplo, 15, 30, etc.).

4. Cuenta del cincuenta al cien de dos en dos (por ejemplo, 50, 52, etc.).

5. Cuenta del sesenta al cien de dos en dos (por ejemplo, 60, 62, etc.).

6. Cuenta del setenta al cien de dos en dos (por ejemplo, 70, 72, etc.).

7. Cuenta del ochenta al cien de dos en dos (por ejemplo, 80, 82, etc.).

8. Cuenta del cien al ochenta de cinco en cinco (por ejemplo, 100, 95, etc.).

9. Cuenta del cien al setenta de dos en dos (por ejemplo, 100, 98, etc.).

10. Cuenta hasta cien de dos en dos (por ejemplo, 2, 4, etc.).

Yo practico

Señorita González is in charge of the stuffed animals that will be given as prizes in the carnival. Each animal has a number. Help señorita González make a list of the prizes. Look at the pictures below and tell her the number attached to each animal.

Yo juego

Señora Lozano always forgets to put something in her children's lunch boxes. Write the word from the list that goes with each picture or number. Then read the word in the box to find out what she forgot.

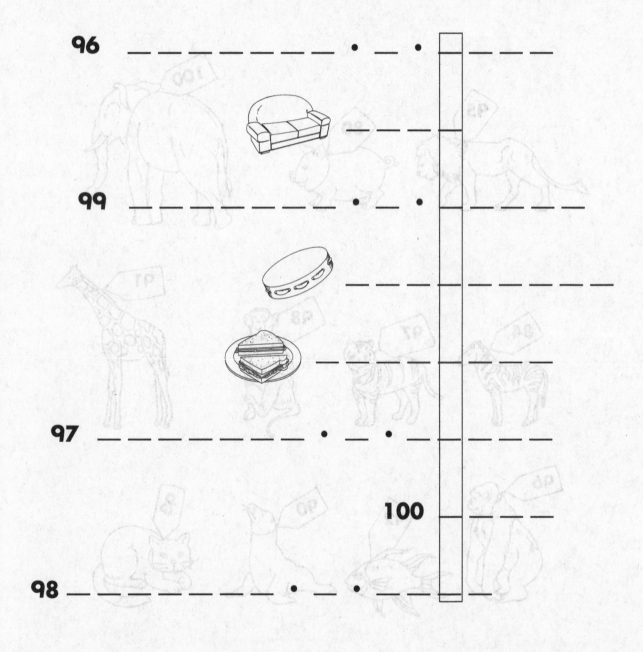

Yo imagino

You are on another planet! The same animals live there as on Earth, but they live in different places, eat different foods, and are different colors and sizes. Draw four of the animals you see and describe them (for example, **La jirafa es morada. Es pequeña. La jirafa come gatos.**). Who in your class can make the animal with the most changes?

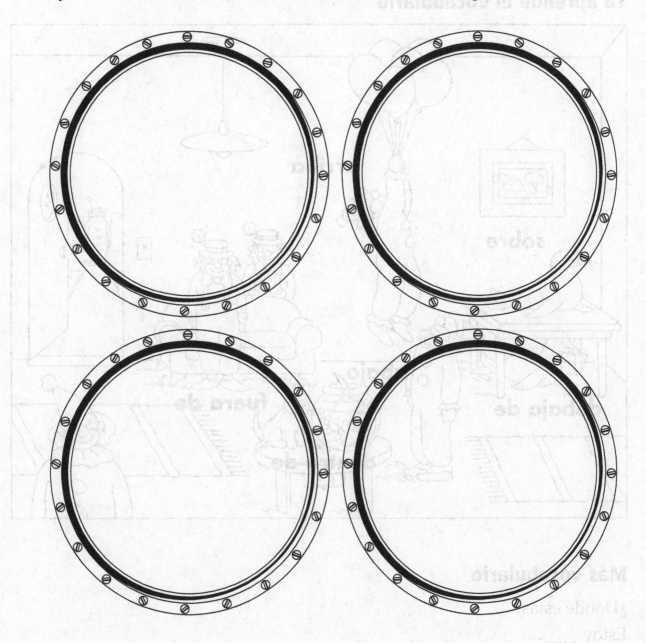

Lección 26

¿Está dentro de, fuera de, arriba o abajo?

Yo aprendo el vocabulario

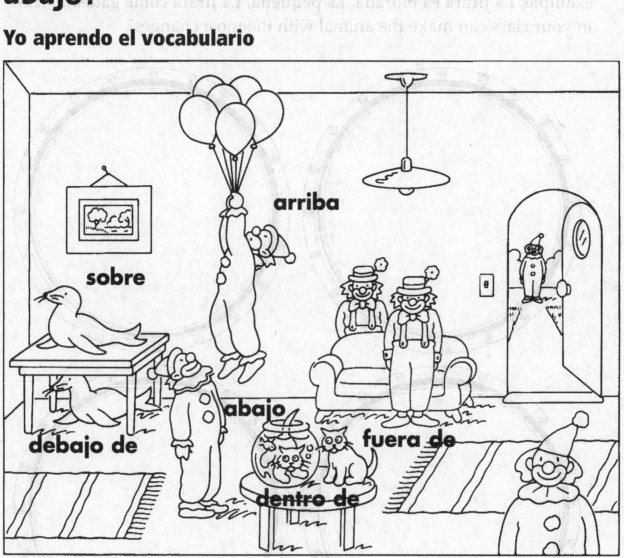

arriba

sobre

debajo de

abajo

dentro de

fuera de

Más vocabulario

¿Dónde estás?

Estoy ____.

Yo hablo

Listen to the questions. Then raise your hand and take turns with your classmates to answer the questions.

1. ¿Está tu casa cerca o lejos de la escuela? _____

2. ¿Está tu casa cerca o lejos del supermercado? _____

3. ¿Dónde está el televisor en la sala de tu casa? _____

4. ¿Pones los zapatos debajo de la cama? _____

5. ¿Qué hay sobre la mesa en la cocina? _____

6. ¿Están tus juguetes o tus muñecas dentro o fuera de tu dormitorio?

_____

7. ¿Qué hay delante de tu pupitre en el salón de clases? _____

8. ¿Qué hay detrás de tu pupitre en el salón de clases? _____

9. ¿Qué hay sobre el escritorio de la maestra o del maestro?

_____

10. ¿Qué hay detrás del escritorio del maestro o de la maestra?

_____

Yo practico

There was a terrible tornado and the Cortina family was thrown everywhere. (Luckily no one was hurt!) Listen to the questions and look at the pictures. Then answer the questions.

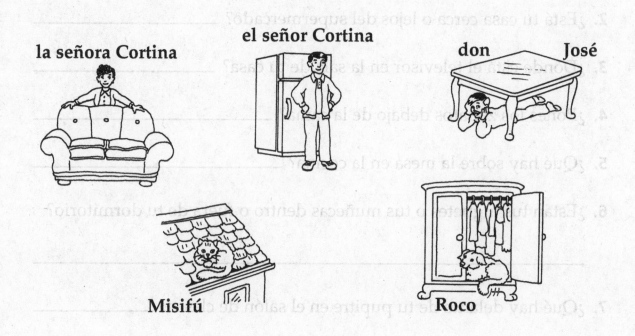

la señora Cortina

el señor Cortina

don   José

Misifú

Roco

1. ¿Dónde está la señora Cortina? _____

2. ¿Dónde está el señor Cortina? _____

3. ¿Dónde está don José? _____

4. ¿Dónde está Misifú? _____

5. ¿Dónde está Roco? _____

Yo juego

The Espinola family is . . . different from most. What are their names?
Listen to the descriptions and see if you can tell. Write the first letter of
each name near their picture.

Yo imagino

Fill the aquarium with make-believe fish. Make each fish different from all the others. Color each fish a different color. Think of six things you can say about your underwater scene. Describe it to your class.

Lección 27

Vamos a practicar todo lo que hemos aprendido

Yo hablo

Marcos wants to know the addresses of the places he will visit today. Look at the map and say the address of each building.

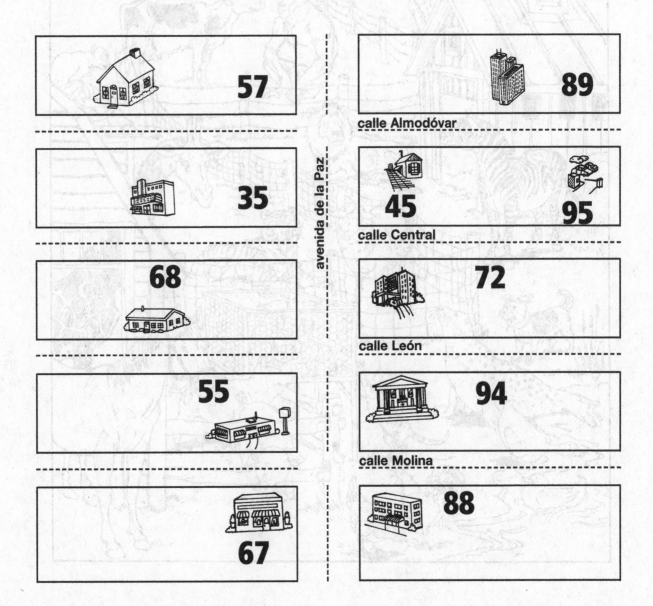

57

89

calle Almodóvar

35

45   **95**

calle Central

68

72

calle León

55

94

calle Molina

67

88

avenida de la Paz

Yo practico

Some animals have escaped from the zoo and wandered into señora Granjera's farmyard. Circle the animals that don't belong on a farm and take turns with your classmates to say the names of the zoo animals.

Yo juego

The names of six sports, six school subjects, and the four seasons of the year are hidden in this puzzle. Find and circle the words. Cross them off the list as you find them in the puzzle.

V	E	R	A	N	O	A	C	N	A	Y	R	B	X	P
B	D	A	R	B	É	I	S	B	O	L	V	F	E	R
A	C	R	T	C	A	S	A	Í	L	I	D	Ú	O	I
L	A	I	E	S	Q	U	I	A	R	E	Ñ	T	T	M
O	M	Ú	S	I	C	A	E	T	A	K	J	B	O	A
N	L	C	H	B	I	N	V	I	E	R	N	O	Ñ	V
C	E	I	L	U	E	S	P	A	Ñ	O	L	L	O	E
E	N	G	U	Z	N	A	D	A	R	H	O	U	M	R
S	P	A	N	D	C	E	L	N	E	V	I	R	U	A
T	R	P	A	T	I	N	A	R	Y	N	O	T	Y	W
O	A	N	O	M	A	T	E	M	Á	T	I	C	A	S
Q	K	U	P	R	S	E	I	N	G	L	É	S	M	O

Six school subjects	Six sports	Four seasons of the year
arte	nadar	primavera
inglés	béisbol	verano
música	patinar	otoño
ciencias	baloncesto	invierno
español	esquiar	
matemáticas	fútbol	

Yo imagino

This Web site has a great selection, but the names of the items are missing. Help your teacher fix the problem so we can e-mail the company.

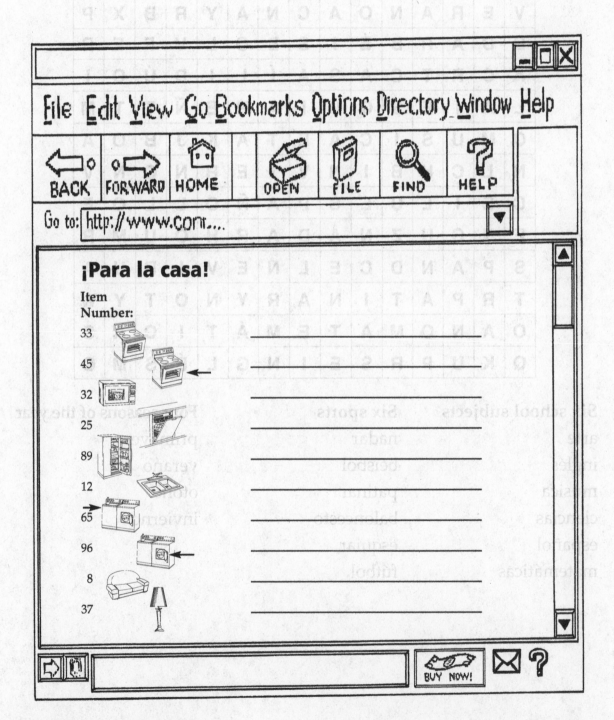

¡Para la familia!

Item
Number:

27

34

20

78

92

44

5

10

85

2

23

Gifts for:

mi mamá _____

mi papá _____

mi hermano _____

mi hermana _____

mi amigo o amiga _____

mis abuelos _____

¡Para mí! _____

End-of-Year Review

Vamos a practicar todo lo que hemos aprendido

Yo hablo

Read the words aloud. Then look at the pictures. Finally, draw a line from each word on the left side of the page to the picture for it on the right side of the page.

las matemáticas

el español

el arte

los estudios sociales

las computadoras

el inglés

la música

las ciencias

el elefante

la cebra

el mono

la jirafa

la foca

el león

el tigre

el gorila

Yo practico

Listen to the instructions. Then look at each set of pictures and follow the instructions.

1.

2.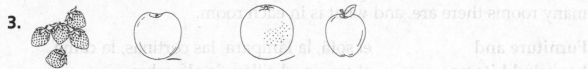

3.

4.

5.

6.

7.

8.

9.

10.

Yo juego

Your parents or guardians just bought a new house. The house is so beautiful and it has so many rooms! It also has a garden and a lovely patio. But you and your family need to move all your furniture, household and home entertainment appliances, and toys to the new house and put them in the right place. Otherwise it would be a huge mess! To help yourself, read the following lists of things you have to move and draw those items where they go in your house. When you are finished, take turns with your classmates describing your houses, how many rooms there are, and what is in each room.

Furniture and household items	el sofá, la lámpara, las cortinas, la cama, el espejo, el sillón, la alfombra, el guardarropas, la computadora
Appliances	la estufa con horno, el microondas, el lavaplatos, el refrigerador, la lavadora, la secadora
Home entertainment and toys	el televisor, el radio, el cartel, los carritos, la muñeca, los juguetes, la bicicleta, los patines, el lector de discos compactos, los discos compactos

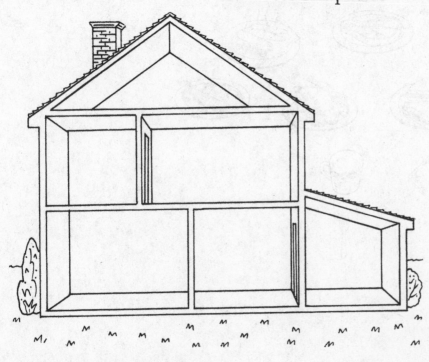

Yo imagino

Make up a story about yourself. Choose from the pictures on this page and the next to make your story serious or silly. Read each sentence and circle a picture to finish the sentence. Then take turns telling the class your story.

Me llamo _____. Tengo _____ años.

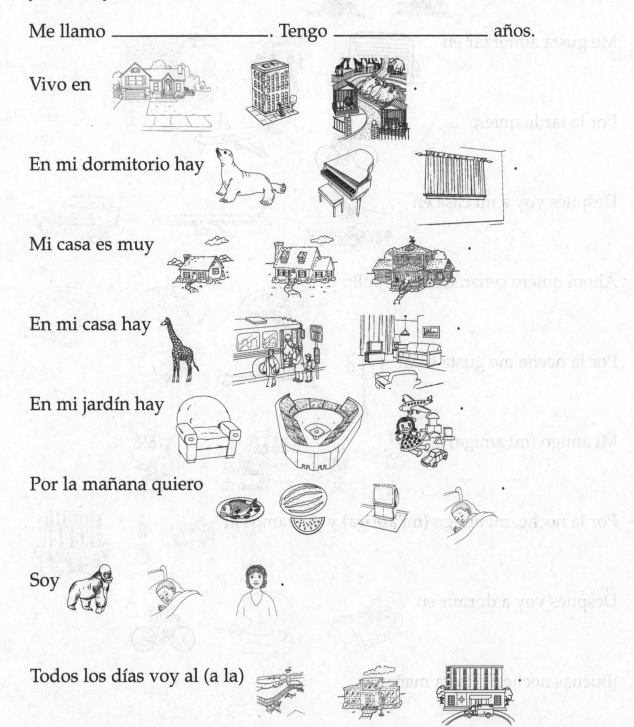

Vivo en

En mi dormitorio hay

Mi casa es muy

En mi casa hay

En mi jardín hay

Por la mañana quiero

Soy

Todos los días voy al (a la)

Me gusta   .

No me gusta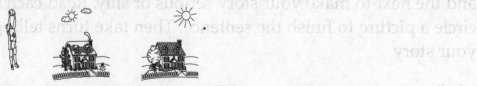

Me gusta almorzar en

Por la tarde quiero    .

Después voy a mi casa en  .

Ahora quiero cenar. Como el pollo y   .

Por la noche me gusta tocar  .

Mi amigo (mi amiga) es   .

Por la noche, mi amigo (mi amiga) y yo vamos al  .

Después voy a dormir en   .

¡Buenas noches! ¡Hasta mañana!

SPANISH–ENGLISH GLOSSARY

A

a to, at
a pie walking, by foot
abajo down
abril April
abuela, la grandmother
abuelo, el grandfather
acá here, over here
   ven acá come here *(command)*
Adiós. Goodbye.
¿adónde? (to) where?
   ¿Adónde vas? Where are you
      going?
aeropuerto, el airport
agosto August
agrupa group *(command)*
agua, el water
ahora now
alfabeto, el alphabet
alfombra, la carpet
almuerzo, el lunch
¡alto! stop *(command)*
alto (-a) tall
amarillo (-a) yellow
amiga, la friend *(f.)*
amigo, el friend *(m.)*
amigos, los friends
anaranjado (-a) orange *(color)*
andar en bicicleta to ride a bicycle
animal, el animal
año, el year
   ¿Cuántos años tienes? How old are
      you?

apartamento, el apartment
aquí here
   ¡Aquí está! Here it is!
   ¡Aquí están! Here they are!
   Aquí viene ____. Here comes ____.
arte, el art
arriba up
arroz, el rice
así, así so-so
ático, el attic
autobús, el bus
avión, el airplane
azul blue

B

bajo (-a) short
baloncesto, el basketball
bandera, la flag
beber to drink
   ¿Qué desea beber? What would
      you like to drink?
béisbol, el baseball
biblioteca, la library
bicicleta, la bicycle
bien well, good
   Estoy bien. I am well.
   muy bien very well, very good
blanco (-a) white
blusa, la blouse
boca, la mouth
bonito (-a) pretty
borrar to erase
   borra erase *(command)*
brazos, los arms

buen, bueno (-a) good

  Buenas noches. Good night.

  Buenas tardes. Good afternoon.

  Buenos días. Good morning.

buscar to look for, search

  busca look for, search (command)

C

caballo, el horse

cabeza, la head

cafetería, la lunchroom, cafeteria

caja, la box

calcetines, los socks

calendario, el calendar

caliente hot

  Está caliente. It's hot.

calor, el heat

  Hace calor. It's hot.

calle, la street

cama, la bed

camarera, la waitress

camarero, el waiter

caminar to walk

camisa, la shirt

camiseta, la T-shirt

campo, el country

canción, la song

cantar to sing

  Canto. I sing.

  Quiero cantar (una canción). I want to sing (a song).

  Vamos a cantar. Let's sing.

cara, la face

carne, la meat

cartel, el poster

carritos, los toy cars

carro, el car

casa, la house

catorce fourteen

cebra, la zebra

cena, la dinner

centro, el downtown

centro comercial, el mall

cerca de near

cerdo, el pig

cereal, el cereal

cerezas, las cherries

cero zero

chaqueta, la jacket

chimenea, la chimney

chocolate, el chocolate

cien one hundred

ciencias, las science

cinco five

cincuenta fifty

  cincuenta y uno . . . cincuenta y nueve fifty-one . . . fifty-nine

cine, el movies

círculo, el circle

ciudad, la city

clarinete, el clarinet

clase, la class

  la clase de _____ _____ class

cocina, la kitchen

cocinera, la cook (f.)

cocinero, el cook (m.)

color, el color

  ¿De qué color es? What color is it?

colorear to color

  colorea color (command)

comedor, el dining room

comer to eat

  comes you eat

  como I eat

  ¿Qué desea comer? What would you like to eat?

¿cómo? how? what?

  ¿Cómo es _____? What is _____ like?

  ¿Cómo estás? How are you?

  ¿Cómo se llama _____? What's the _____'s name?

¿Cómo se llama? What's your (formal)/his/her name?

¿Cómo te llamas? What's your (familiar) name?

computadora, la computer

con with

conejo, el rabbit

contar to count

cuenta count (*command*)

Vamos a contar. Let's count.

contento (-a) happy

Estoy contento (-a). I'm happy.

cortinas, las curtains

creyón, el crayon

cruzar to cross

Cruzo la calle. I cross the street.

cuadrado, el square

¿cuál? what? which?

¿Cuál falta? Which (one) is missing? What's missing?

¿cuándo? when?

¿Cuándo comes ___? When do you eat ___?

¿Cuándo es tu (su) cumpleaños? When is your birthday?

¿cuántos (–as)? how many?

¿Cuántos/Cuántas (días, semanas, meses) hay? How many (days, weeks, months) are there?

¿Cuántos años tiene? How old is he/she/it?

¿Cuántos años tienes? How old are you?

¿Cuántos tengo? How many do I have?

cuarenta forty

cuarenta y uno . . . cuarenta y nueve forty-one . . . forty-nine

cuarto, el room

cuarto de baño, el bathroom

cuatro four

cuchara, la spoon

cuchillo, el knife

cumpleaños, el birthday

¿Cuándo es tu (su) cumpleaños? When is your birthday?

Mi cumpleaños es el ___ de ___. My birthday is the ___ of ___.

D

dar to give

dale give him/her (*command*)

dame give me (*command*)

dar un saltito to hop

da un saltito hop (*command*)

date una vuelta turn around once (*command*)

de of, from

De nada. You're welcome.

debajo de under

decir to say

Dice «___». He/She/It says ___.

dice he/she/it says

dicen they say

¿Qué dice ___? What does ___ say?

dedos, los fingers

delante de in front of

delgado (-a) thin

dentro de inside

derecha, la right (*direction*)

Miro a la derecha. I look to the right.

desayuno, el breakfast

desear to want

Deseo ___. I would like ___.

despacio slowly

detrás de behind

día, el day

　Buenos días. Good morning.

　¿Qué día es hoy? What day is
　today?

dibujar to draw

　dibuja draw (command)

　dibuja una línea draw a line
　(command)

　Dibujo. I draw.

diciembre December

diecinueve nineteen

dieciocho eighteen

dieciséis sixteen

diecisiete seventeen

diez ten

director, el principal (m.)

directora, la principal (f.)

disco compacto, el CD

doce twelve

domingo, el Sunday

¿dónde? where

　¿Dónde está ____? Where is ____?

　¿Dónde están ____? Where are
　____?

　¿Dónde estás? Where are you?

dormir to sleep

dormitorio, el bedroom

dos two

durazno, el peach

duro (-a) hard

E

edificio, el building

educación física, la physical
　education

el the

él he

elefante, el elephant

elige choose (command)

ella she

en in, on, into, at

enero January

enfermera, la nurse (f.)

enfermero, el nurse (m.)

enojado (-a) angry

　Estoy enojado (-a). I'm angry.

entrada, la entrance

Es ____. It's ____.; He/She/It is ____.

Es el (la) ____. It's the ____.

Es un (una) ____. It's a ____.

escritorio, el desk

escuchar to listen

　escucha listen (command)

　escucho I listen

　Escucho música en ____. I listen to
　music on ____.

escuela, la school

español, el Spanish

espejo, el mirror

esperar to wait

　espera wait (command)

esquiar to ski

esta, este this

estacionamiento, el parking lot

estación de trenes, la train station

estadio, el stadium

estar to be

　está he/she/it is

　¿Está ____? Is he/she/it ____?

　Está en ____. He/She/It is in
　____.

　Está lloviendo. It's raining.

　Está nevando. It's snowing.

　están you are, they are

　Están en ____. They are in ____.

　estás you are

　¿Dónde estás? Where are you?

　estoy I am, I'm

　Estoy ____. I'm ____.

　Estoy (muy) bien. I'm (very) well.

　Estoy (muy) mal. I feel (very)
　bad.

Estoy así, así. I'm so-so.

Estoy contento (-a). I'm happy.

Estoy enojado (-a). I'm angry.

Estoy más o menos. I'm okay, more or less.

Estoy pensando en . . . I'm thinking of . . .

Estoy triste. I'm sad.

estudiar to study

Estudio. I study.

estudios sociales, los social studies

estufa, la stove

F

falda, la skirt

familia, la family

febrero February

fecha, la date (*calendar*)

¿Qué fecha es hoy? What's the date?

feo (-a) ugly

fiesta, la party

figura, la shape

flauta, la flute

foca, la seal

fregadero, el sink

fresas, las strawberries

frío (-a) cold (*adjective*)

frío, el cold (*noun*)

Hace frío. It's cold.

Tengo frío. I'm cold.

fuera de outside

fútbol, el soccer

fútbol americano, el football

G

gafas de sol, las sunglasses

galletas, las crackers

gallina, la hen

gallo, el rooster

garaje, el garage

gato, el cat

gimnasio, el gym

gimnasia, hacer to do gymnastics

globo, el globe

gordo (-a) fat

gorila, el gorilla

Gracias. Thank you.

grande large

granja, la farm

gris gray

guardarropas, el wardrobe, closet

guardián, el zookeeper

guitarra, la guitar

gustar to like

Me gusta ____. I like (*s.*) ____.

Me gustan ____. I like (*pl.*) ____.

No me gusta ____. I don't like (*s.*) ____.

No me gustan ____. I don't like (*pl.*) ____.

No, no me gusta. No, I don't like it. (*s.*)

Sí, me gusta. Yes, I like it. (*s.*)

Sí, me gustan. Yes, I like them. (*pl.*)

¿Te gusta ____? Do you like (*s.*) ____?

¿Te gustan ____? Do you like (*pl.*) ____?

¿Qué te gusta? What do you like?

H

hablar to speak

Hablo por teléfono. I'm talking on the telephone.

hacer to make, to do

Hace ____. It's ____.

Hace buen tiempo. The weather is good.

Hace calor. It's hot.

Hace frío. It's cold.

Hace mal tiempo. The weather is bad.

Hace sol. It's sunny.

Hace viento. It's windy.

¿Qué haces? What are you doing?

¿Qué va a hacer? What is he/she going to do?

¿Qué vas a hacer? What are you (familiar) going to do?

¿Qué va a hacer usted? What are you (formal) going to do?

hacer gimnasia to do gymnastics

hacer un viaje to take a trip

Hago ejercicios. I exercise.

hasta until, to

¡Hasta la vista! See you later.

¡Hasta luego! See you later.

¡Hasta mañana! See you tomorrow!

¡Hasta pronto! See you soon!

hay there is, there are

hermana, la sister

hermanastra, la stepsister

hermanastro, el stepbrother

hermano, el brother

hija, la daughter

hijastra, la stepdaughter

hijastro, el stepson

hijo, el son

¡Hola! Hello!, Hi!

hora hour

hora de recreo, la recess

horno, el oven

hospital, el hospital

hoy today

Hoy es ____. Today is ____.

Hoy es el ____. Today is the ____.

¿Qué día es hoy? What day is today?

I

inglés, el English

instrumento, el instrument

instrumentos musicales, los musical instruments

invierno, el winter

ir to go

¿Adónde vas? Where are you going?

¿Qué va a hacer? What is he/she/it going to do?

¿Qué vas a hacer? What are you (familiar) going to do?

¿Qué va a hacer? What are you (formal) going to do?

Va a ____. He/She/It is going to ____.

Vamos a ____. Let's ____.

ve go (command)

Voy a ____. I'm going to ____.

Voy a ____ en (a) ____. I'm going to ____ by ____.

Voy a jugar al ____. I'm going to play ____.

ir de picnic to go on a picnic

izquierda, la left (direction)

Miro a la izquierda. I look to the left.

J

jardín, el garden

jirafa, la giraffe

jueves, el Thursday

jugar to play (a game)

juego I play

Voy a jugar al ____. I'm going to play ____.

jugo, el   juice

   el jugo de (____) (____) juice

juguetes, los   toys

julio   July

junio   June

L

la   the

lámpara, la   lamp

lápiz, el   pencil

las   the (f. pl.)

lástima   pity

   ¡Que lástima!   What a pity!

lavadora, la   washing machine

lavaplatos, el   dishwasher

leche, la   milk

lechuga, la   lettuce

lector de discos compactos, el   CD
   player

leer   to read

   Leo.   I read.

lejos de   far

león, el   lion

letra, la   letter

levántate   stand up (command)

libro, el   book

limón, el   lemon

limpio (-a)   clean

lindo (-a)   pretty

llamarse   to be called, named

   me llamo   my name is

   se llama   his/her/its, your (formal)
     name is

   te llamas   your name is

llevar   to wear

   lleva   he, she is wearing, you're
     (formal) wearing

   llevas   you're (familiar) wearing

llevo   I'm wearing

¿Qué llevas?   What are you
   wearing? What do you have on?

llover   to rain

   Está lloviendo.   It's raining.

lobo, el   wolf

los   the (m. pl.)

luego   later

lunes, el   Monday

luz, la   light

   luces, las   lights (pl.)

M

madrastra, la   stepmother

madre, la   mother

maestra, la   teacher (f.)

maestro, el   teacher (m.)

mal; malo (-a)   bad; not well

   Estoy (muy) mal.   I feel (very) bad.

mamá, la   mom

manos, las   hands

manzana, la   apple

mañana, la   morning; tomorrow

   Hasta mañana.   See you tomorrow.

   Mañana es ____.   Tomorrow is ____.

mapa, el   map

marcador, el   marker

marrón   brown

martes, el   Tuesday

marzo   March

matemáticas, las   mathematics

mayo   May

mediano (-a)   medium

menú, el   menu

mes, el; meses, los   month; months

mesa, la   table

mi, mis   my

microondas, el   microwave

miércoles, el   Wednesday

mirar to look

  mira look *(command)*

  Miro a la derecha. I look to the right.

  Miro a la izquierda. I look to the left.

mono, el monkey

morado (-a) purple

mostrar to show

  muéstrame show me *(command)*

mucho (-a) much

muñeca, la doll

museo, el museum

música, la music

muy very

N

nadar to swim

naranja, la orange *(fruit)*

nariz, la nose

negro (-a) black

nevar to snow

  Está nevando. It's snowing.

niña, la girl

niño, el boy

niños, los children

no no

No hay ____. There is (are) no ____.

noche, la night

  Buenas noches. Good night.

noventa ninety

  noventa y uno . . . noventa y nueve
    ninety-one . . . ninety-nine

noviembre November

nueve nine

nuevo (-a) new

número, el number

  ¿Qué número es? What number is
    it?

O

o or

octágono, el octagon

octubre October

ochenta eighty

  ochenta y uno . . . ochenta y nueve
    eighty-one . . . eighty-nine

ocho eight

oficina, la office

ojos, los eyes

once eleven

orejas, las ears

oso, el bear

otoño, el fall, autumn

oveja, la sheep

P

padrastro, el stepfather

padre, el father

pájaro, el bird

pan tostado, el toast

pandereta, la tambourine

pantalones cortos, los shorts

pantalones, los pants

papá, el dad

papa, la potato

papel, el paper

para for, to

parada de autobús, la bus stop

parque, el park

patinar skate

patio, el patio

patio de recreo, el playground

pato, el duck

peces, los fish (pl.)

pelo, el hair

pensar to think

  Estoy pensando en . . . I'm thinking of . . .

pequeño (-a) small

pera, la pear

perro, el dog

persona, la person

personas, las people

pescado, el fish (edible)

pescar to fish

pez, el fish (s.)

piano, el piano

piernas, las legs

pies, los feet

pijama, el pajamas

Pinto. I paint.

piña, la pineapple

piscina, la swimming pool

pizarrón, el chalkboard

plátano, el banana

plato, el plate

playa, la beach

pobre poor

  pobrecito poor thing

policía, el police officer (m.)

policía, la police officer (f.)

pollo, el chicken

poner to put

  pon put (command)

  Pon un círculo. Draw a circle. (command)

  Pon una X. Draw an X. (command)

  pongo I put

poner la mesa to set the table

  Pongo la mesa. I set the table.

por for, by, through

  Por favor. Please.

practicar to practice

primavera, la spring

primero first

puerta, la door

pupitre, el student desk

que who; which, that

¿qué? what?

  ¿De qué color es? What color is it?

  ¿Qué desea beber? What would you (formal) like to drink?

  ¿Qué desea comer? What would you (formal) like to eat?

  ¿Qué día es hoy? What day is today?

  ¿Qué dice ____? What does ____ say?

  ¿Qué eres? What are you?

  ¿Qué es? What is this?

  ¿Qué fecha es hoy? What's the date?

  ¿Qué figura es? What shape is it?

  ¿Qué haces? What are you doing?

  ¿Qué llevas? What are you wearing? What do you have on?

  ¿Qué número es? What number is it?

  ¿Qué quieres comer? What do you want to eat?

  ¿Qué quieres hacer? What do you want to do?

  ¿Qué son? What are these?

  ¿Qué tal? What's up? How's it going? How are they?

  ¿Qué tiempo hace? What's the weather like?

  ¿Qué tiene ____? What does ____ have?

  ¿Qué va a hacer? What is he, she, it going to do?

  ¿Qué vas a hacer? What are you going to do?

¡qué! how! what!

  ¡Qué bonito (-a)! How pretty.

  ¡Qué bueno! How wonderful!

  ¡Qué lástima! What a pity! What a shame!

  ¡Qué rico! Delicious!

querer to want

  ¿Qué quieres comer? What do you want to eat?

  quieres you want

  quiero I want

queso, el cheese

¿quién? who?

  ¿Quién es? Who is it?

  ¿Quién tiene ___? Who has ___?

quince fifteen

quita take (command)

R

radio, la radio (broadcast)

radio, el radio (device)

rana, la frog

rápido (-a) fast

rápido quickly

rascacielos, el skyscraper

ratón, el mouse

rectángulo, el rectangle

refrigerador, el refrigerator

regla, la ruler

reloj, el clock

restaurante, el restaurant

rico rich

rojo (-a) red

rosado (-a) pink

S

sábado, el Saturday

sacar to take out, remove

saca take out, remove (command)

  Saco. I take.

sala, la living room

sala de estar, la living room

salida, la exit

salón de clases, el classroom

saltar to jump

  salta jump (command)

saltar la cuerda jump rope, to

sandía, la watermelon

sándwich, el sandwich

Se llama ___. His/Her/Its name is ___.

secadora, la dryer

secretaria, la secretary (f.)

secretario, el secretary (m.)

seis six

semáforo, el traffic light

semana, la week

sentarse to sit down

  siéntate sit down (command)

sentir to feel

  Lo siento. I'm sorry.

señor Mr.

señora Mrs.

señorita Miss

septiembre September

ser to be

  es he/she/it is, you (formal) are

  son they are

  soy I am

servilleta, la napkin

sesenta sixty

  sesenta y uno . . . sesenta y nueve sixty-one . . . sixty-nine

setenta seventy

  setenta y uno . . . setenta y nueve seventy-one . . . seventy-nine

sí yes

siete seven

sigue go (command)

silla, la chair

sillón, el   armchair

sobre   on (on top of)

sofá, el   sofa

sombrero, el   hat

sopa, la   soup

sótano, el   basement

suave   soft, smooth

sucio (-a)   dirty

supermercado, el   supermarket

su, sus   his, her, its; your; their

suéter, el   sweater

T

también   also, too

tambor, el   drum

tarde, la   afternoon

  Buenas tardes.   Good afternoon.

taza, la   cup

techo, el   roof

teléfono, el   telephone

teléfono celular, el   cellular telephone

televisor, el   television set (furniture)

televisión, la   television (broadcast)

tenedor, el   fork

tener   to have

  tengo   I have

    Tengo ____ años.   I'm ____ years old.

    Tengo calor.   I'm hot.

    Tengo dolor.   I hurt. I'm in pain. I have a pain.

    Tengo frío.   I'm cold.

    Tengo hambre.   I'm hungry.

    Tengo miedo.   I'm afraid. I'm scared.

    Tengo prisa.   I'm in a hurry.

    Tengo sed.   I'm thirsty.

    Tengo sueño.   I'm sleepy.

    Tengo suerte.   I'm lucky.

tiene   he/she/it has

Tiene ____ años.   He/She is ____ years old. You are ____ years old.

tienes   you have

  ¿Tienes ____?   Do you have ____?

tenis, el   tennis

tiempo, el   weather

  Hace buen tiempo.   The weather is good.

  Hace mal tiempo.   The weather is bad.

  ¿Qué tiempo hace?   What's the weather like?

tienda, la   store

tigre, el   tiger

títere, el   puppet

tiza, la   chalk

tocar   to touch

  toca   touch (command)

tocar   to play (an instrument)

  Quiero tocar ____.   I want to play ____.

toma   take (command)

tomate, el   tomato

tostado, el pan   toast

tráeme   bring me (command)

traje de baño, el   bathing suit

trece   thirteen

treinta   thirty

  treinta y uno . . . treinta y nueve   thirty-one . . . thirty-nine

tren, el   train

tres   three

triángulo, el   triangle

triste   sad

  Estoy triste.   I'm sad.

trompeta, la   trumpet

tu, tus   your

tú   you (familiar)

U

un, una   a, an
un, uno, una   one
usted   you (formal)
ustedes   you (*pl.*)
uvas, las   grapes

V

Va a ____.   He/She/It is going to ____.
vaca, la   cow
Vamos a ____.   Let's ____.
vaso, el   glass
ve   go, walk (to) (*command*)
ver   to see
   veo   I see, I watch
veinte   twenty
   veintiuno . . . veintinueve   twenty-
   one . . . twenty-nine
venir   to come
   Aquí viene ____.   Here comes ____.
   ven acá   come here (*command*)
ventana, la   window
ver   to see, to watch
   veo   I see, I watch
verano, el   summer

verde   green
vestido, el   dress
viaje, el   trip
   hacer un viaje   to take a trip
viento   wind
viernes, el   Friday
violín, el   violin
vivir   to live
   Vivo en ____.   I live in ____.
Voy a la (al) ____ en (a) ____.   I'm
   going ____ by ____.
Voy a la (al) ____.   I'm going to ____.
Voy a jugar al ____.   I'm going to play
   ____.

Y

y   and
ya   already
yo   I

Z

zanahorias, las   carrots
zapatos, los   shoes
zoológico, el   zoo

ENGLISH–SPANISH GLOSSARY

A

a un, una
above sobre
afternoon la tarde
  Good afternoon. Buenas
    tardes.
airplane el avión
airport el aeropuerto
alphabet el alfabeto
already ya
also también
an un, una
and y
angry enojado (-a)
  I'm angry. Estoy enojado (-a).
animal el animal
apartment el apartamento
apple la manzana
April abril
are está, están, es, son
  Are there ___? ¿Hay ___?
  How are you? ¿Cómo estás?
    ¿Cómo está usted?
  there are hay
  There are no ___. No hay
    ___.
armchair el sillón
arms los brazos
art el arte
at a, en

B

attic el ático
August agosto
autumn el otoño

bad; badly mal; malo
  I feel bad. Estoy mal.
banana el plátano
baseball el béisbol
basement el sótano
basketball el baloncesto
bathing suit el traje de baño
bathroom el cuarto de baño
bear el oso
bed la cama
bedroom el dormitorio
be, to estar, ser
  he, she, it is es; está
  I am estoy; soy
  they are están; son
  you are estás (*familiar*); está
    (*formal*); eres (*familiar*); es
    (*formal*)
beach la playa
behind detrás de
bicycle la bicicleta
bird el pájaro
birthday el cumpleaños
  My birthday is the ___ of ___.
    Mi cumpleaños es el ___
    de ___.

When is your birthday?
¿Cuándo es tu cumpleaños?
black negro (-a)
blouse la blusa
blue azul
book el libro
box la caja
boy el niño
breakfast el desayuno
bring me tráeme (*command*)
brother el hermano
brown marrón
building el edificio
bus el autobús
bus stop la parada de autobús
by por

C

cafeteria la cafetería
calendar el calendario
called, to be llamarse
car el carro
carpet la alfombra
carrots las zanahorias
cat el gato
CD el disco compacto
CD player el lector
  de discos compactos
cellular telephone el teléfono
  celular
cereal el cereal
chair la silla
chalk la tiza
chalkboard el pizarrón
cheese el queso

cherries las cerezas
chicken el pollo
child el niño, la niña
children los niños
chimney la chimenea
chocolate el chocolate
choose elige (*command*)
circle el círculo
city la ciudad
  in the city en la ciudad
clarinet el clarinete
class la clase
classroom el salón de clases
clean limpio (-a)
clock el reloj
cold (*adjective*) frío, (-a)
cold (*noun*) el frío
  I'm cold. Tengo frío.
  It's cold. Hace frío.
color el color
  What color is it? ¿De qué
  color es?
color, to colorear
  color colorea (*command*)
come venir
  Here comes ____. Aquí
  viene ____.
  come here ven acá (*command*)
computer la computadora
cook la cocinera (*f.*),
  el cocinero (*m.*)
count, to contar
  count cuenta (*command*)
  Let's count. Vamos a contar.
country el campo
  in the country en el campo

cow   la vaca
crackers   las galletas
crayon   el creyón
cross, to   cruzar
  cross   cruza (*command*)
  I cross the street.   Cruzo la calle.
cup   la taza
curtains   las cortinas

D

dad   el papá
date   la fecha
  What is the date?   ¿Qué fecha es hoy?
daughter   la hija
day   el día
  the days of the week   los días de la semana
  What day is today?   ¿Qué día es hoy?
December   diciembre
desk   el escritorio
dining room   el comedor
dinner   la cena
dirty   sucio (-a)
dishwasher   el lavaplatos
do, to   hacer
  What are you doing?   ¿Qué haces? ¿Qué hace usted?
  What are you going to do?
    ¿Qué vas a hacer? ¿Qué va a hacer usted?
  What is he/she/it going to do?   ¿Qué va a hacer?

dog   el perro
doll   la muñeca
door   la puerta
down   abajo
downtown   el centro
draw, to   dibujar
  I draw.   Dibujo.
  Draw a line.   Dibuja una línea. (*command*)
  Draw a circle.   Pon un círculo. (*command*)
  Draw an X.   Pon una X. (*command*)
dress   el vestido
drink, to   beber
  What would you like to drink?   ¿Qué desea beber?
drum   el tambor
dryer   la secadora
duck   el pato

E

ears   las orejas
eat, to   comer
  I eat   como
  What would you like to eat?   ¿Qué desea comer?
  you eat   comes
eight   ocho
eighteen   dieciocho
eighty   ochenta
  eighty-one . . . eighty-nine   ochenta y uno . . . ochenta y nueve

elephant   el elefante
eleven   once
English   el inglés
entrance   la entrada
erase, to   borrar
  erase   borra (command)
exit   la salida
eyes   los ojos

F

face   la cara
fall (season)   el otoño
family   la familia
far   lejos de
farm   la granja
fast   rápido (-a)
fat   gordo (-a)
father   el padre, el papá
  stepfather   el padrastro
February   febrero
feel, to   sentir
  I'm very sorry.   Lo siento
    mucho.
  I feel (very) bad.   Estoy (muy)
    mal.
feet   los pies
fifteen   quince
fifty   cincuenta
  fifty-one . . . fifty-nine
    cincuenta y uno . . . cincuenta
    y nueve
fingers   los dedos
first   primero (-a)
fish   el pez, los peces
five   cinco
flag   la bandera

flute   la flauta
football   el fútbol americano
for   para, por
fork   el tenedor
forty   cuarenta
  forty-one . . . forty-
    nine   cuarenta y uno . . . .
    cuarenta y nueve
four   cuatro
fourteen   catorce
Friday   el viernes
friend(s)   la amiga (f.), el amigo
    (m.), los amigos (pl.)
frog   la rana
from   de

G

garage   el garaje
garden   el jardín
giraffe   la jirafa
girl   la niña
give, to   dar
  give him/her/it   dale (command)
  give me   dame (command)
glass   el vaso
globe   el globo
go, to   ir
  go   sigue, ve (command)
  I'm going to ___.   Voy a ___.
  I'm going to ___ by ___.   Voy
    a ___ en (a) ___.
  What are you going to do?
    ¿Qué vas a hacer? ¿Qué va a
    hacer usted?

What is he/she/it going to do? ¿Qué va a hacer?

Where are you going? ¿Adónde vas? ¿Adónde va usted?

go bike riding, to montar en bicicleta

go on a picnic ir de picnic

good bien

I am good. Estoy bien.

good bueno

Good afternoon. Buenas tardes.

Good morning. Buenos días.

Good night. Buenas noches.

Goodbye. Adiós.

gorilla el gorila

grandfather el abuelo

grandmother la abuela

grapes las uvas

gray gris

green verde

group, to agrupar

group agrupa (*command*), agrupen (*pl. command*)

guitar la guitarra

gym el gimnasio

H

hair el pelo

hands las manos

happy contento

I'm happy. Estoy contento (-a)

hard duro (-a)

hat sombrero

have, to tener

I have tengo

he/she/it has tiene

you have tienes (*familiar*), tiene (*formal*)

Who has ___? ¿Quién tiene?

he él

head la cabeza

hello hola

hen la gallina

her su, sus

here aquí, acá

Come here. Ven acá.

Here comes ___. Aquí viene ___.

Here it is! ¡Aquí está!

Here they are! ¡Aquí están!

hi hola

his su, sus

hop da un saltito (*command*)

horse el caballo

hospital el hospital

hot caliente

It's hot. Está caliente. Hace calor. (*weather expression*)

house la casa

how? ¿cómo?

How are you? ¿Cómo estás? ¿Cómo está usted?

How old are you? ¿Cuántos años tienes?

How old is he/she/it? ¿Cuántos años tiene?

how! ¡qué!

How pretty! ¡Qué bonito (-a)!

How wonderful! ¡Qué bueno!

how many? ¿cuántos (-as)?

How many do I have? ¿Cuántos tengo?

I

I   yo
   I'm afraid.   Tengo miedo.
   I'm angry.   Estoy enojado (-a).
   I'm cold.   Tengo frío.
   I'm happy.   Estoy contento (-a).
   I'm hot.   Tengo calor.
   I'm hungry.   Tengo hambre.
   I'm in a hurry.   Tengo prisa.
   **I'm in pain. I have a pain. I
      hurt.**   Tengo dolor.
   I'm lucky.   Tengo suerte.
   I'm not (very) well.   No estoy
      (muy) bien.
   I'm sad.   Estoy triste.
   I'm scared.   Tengo miedo.
   I'm sleepy.   Tengo sueño.
   I'm so-so.   Estoy así, así.
   I'm thirsty.   Tengo sed.
   I'm (very) well.   Estoy
      (muy) bien.
   I'm ___ years old.   Tengo ___
      años.
in   en
in front of   delante de
inside   dentro de
instrument   el instrumento
into   en
is   es, está
   Is there ___?   ¿Hay ___?
There is ___.   Hay ___.
There is no ___.   No hay ___.

J

jacket   la chaqueta
January   enero
juice   el jugo
July   julio
jump, to   saltar
   jump   salta (*command*)
jump rope, to   saltar la cuerda
June   junio

K

kitchen   la cocina
knife   el cuchillo

L

lamp   lámpara
large   grande
later   luego
left (*direction*)   la izquierda
legs   las piernas
lemon   el limón
Let's ___.   Vamos a ___.
   Let's count.   Vamos a contar.
   Let's sing.   Vamos a cantar.
letter   la letra
lettuce   la lechuga
library   la biblioteca
light   la luz
lion   el león
living room   la sala, la
   sala de estar

look, to   mirar
   I look to the left.   Miro a la
     izquierda.
   I look to the right.   Miro a la
     derecha.
   look   mira (command)
look for   busca (command)
lunch   almuerzo, el
lunchroom   la cafetería

M

make, to   hacer
mall   el centro comercial
many   muchos (-as)
   How many?   ¿Cuántos (-as)?
map   el mapa
March   marzo
marker   el marcador
mathematics   las matemáticas
May   mayo
me   me; mí
meat   la carne
medium   mediano (-a)
menu   el menú
microwave   el microondas
milk   la leche
mirror   el espejo
Miss   señorita
mom   la mamá
Monday   el lunes
monkey   el mono
month; months   el mes;
   los meses
morning   la mañana
   Good morning.   Buenos días.

mother   la madre
   stepmother   la madrastra
mouse   el ratón
mouth   la boca
movie theater   el cine
Mr.   señor
Mrs.   señora
much   mucho (-a)
museum   el museo
music   la música
my   mi, mis

N

named, to be   llamarse
   his/her name is   se llama
   my name is   me llamo
   your name is   te llamas
   What's you name?   ¿Cómo te
     llamas?
   What's his, her, its
     name?   ¿Cómo se llama?
napkin   la servilleta
near   cerca de
new   nuevo (-a)
night   la noche
   Good night.   Buenas noches.
nine   nueve
nineteen   diecinueve
ninety   noventa
   ninety-one . . . ninety nine
     noventa y uno . . . noventa y
     nueve
no   no
nose   la nariz
not   no

not well mal, malo
November noviembre
now ahora
number el número
> **What number is this?** ¿Qué número es?

nurse el enfermero *(m.)*, la enfermera *(f.)*

O

octagon el octágono
October octubre
of de
office la oficina
on en
one un, uno, una
one hundred cien
or o
orange *(color)* anaranjado (-a)
orange *(fruit)* la naranja
outside fuera de
oven el horno
over here acá

P

pain el dolor
> **I'm in pain. I have a ___ pain.** Tengo dolor.

pajamas el pijama
pants los pantalones
paper el papel
park el parque
parking lot el estacionamiento
party la fiesta

patio el patio
peach el durazno
pear la pera
pencil el lápiz
people las personas, la gente
person la persona
physical education la educación física
piano el piano
pig el cerdo
pineapple la piña
pink rosado (-a)
pity lástima
> **What a pity!** ¡Qué lástima!

plate el plato
play, to (a game) jugar
> **I'm going to play ___.** Voy a jugar al ___.

playground el patio de recreo
please por favor
police officer el policía, la policía
poor pobre
> **poor thing** pobrecito (-a)

poster el cartel
pretty bonito (-a)
principal el director, la directora
puppet el títere
purple morado (-a)
put, to poner
> **put** pon (command)

Q

quick *(adjective)* rápido (-a)
quickly *(adverb)* rápido

R

rabbit el conejo
radio el radio (*appliance*), la radio (*broadcast*)
rain, to llover
  It's raining. Está lloviendo.
read, to leer
recess la hora de recreo
rectangle el rectángulo
red rojo (-a)
rice el arroz
ride a bike, to andar en bicicleta
right (*direction*) la derecha
  I look to the right. Miro a la derecha.
roof el techo
room(s) el cuarto, los cuartos
rooster el gallo
ruler la regla

S

sad triste
  I'm sad Estoy triste.
sandwich el sándwich
Saturday el sábado
say, to decir
  he/she/it says dice
  He/She/It says, "___."
    Dice «___».
  they say dicen
  What does ___ say? ¿Qué dice ___?
school la escuela

science las ciencias
seal la foca
search busca (*command*)
secretary el secretario, la secretaria
See you later! ¡Hasta la vista! ¡Hasta luego!
See you soon! ¡Hasta pronto!
See you tomorrow! ¡Hasta mañana!
September septiembre
set the table poner la mesa
seven siete
seventeen diecisiete
seventy setenta
  seventy-one . . . seventy-nine setenta y uno . . . setenta y nueve
shape la figura
she ella
sheep la oveja
shirt la camisa
shoes los zapatos
short bajo (-a)
shorts los pantalones cortos
show, to mostrar
  show me muéstrame (*command*)
sing, to cantar
  I sing. Canto.
  I want to sing (a song). Quiero cantar (una canción).
  Let's sing. Vamos a cantar.
sink el fregadero
sister la hermana
  stepsister la hermanastra
sit down, to sentarse

sit down   siéntate (command)

six   seis

sixteen   dieciséis

sixty   sesenta

  sixty-one . . . sixty-nine
    sesenta y uno . . . sesenta y
    nueve

skate   patinar

ski, to   esquiar

skinny   flaco (-a)

skirt   la falda

skyscraper   el rascacielos

sleep, to   dormir

sleepy, to be   tener sueño

  I'm sleepy.   Tengo sueño.

slowly   despacio

small   pequeño (-a)

smooth   suave

snow, to   nevar

  It's snowing.   Está nevando.

so-so   así, así

  I'm so-so.   Estoy así, así.

soccer   el fútbol

social studies   los estudios
    sociales

socks   los calcetines

sofa   el sofá

soft   suave

son   el hijo

song   la canción

sorry, to be   sentir

  I'm (very) sorry.   Lo siento
    (mucho).

soup   la sopa

Spanish   el español

speak, to   hablar

spoon   la cuchara

spring   la primavera

square   el cuadrado

stadium   el estadio

stepbrother   el hermanastro

stepdaughter   la hijastra

stepfather   el padrastro

stepmother   la madrastra

stepsister   la hermanastra

stepson   el hijastro

Stop!   ¡Alto! (command)

store   la tienda

stove   la estufa

strawberries   las fresas

street   la calle

student desk   el pupitre

study, to   estudiar

  I study   estudio

summer   el verano

sun   el sol

  It's sunny.   Hace sol.

Sunday   el domingo

sunglasses   las gafas de sol

supermarket   el supermercado

sweater   el suéter

swim, to   nadar

swimming pool   la piscina

T

table   la mesa

take, to   tomar

take away   quita (command)

take a trip, to   hacer un viaje

talk, to   hablar

  I'm talking on the telephone.
    Hablo por teléfono.

tall   alto (-a)